All about English Words

WORD PERFECT
BOOK EIGHT

BY

RONALD RIDOUT

ILLUSTRATED BY

GEORGE W. ADAMSON, M.S.I.A.

Ginn and Company Ltd
LONDON AND AYLESBURY

BOOKS BY THE SAME AUTHOR

Write in English, Books 1-8: a new style of English Workbook providing a carefully graded course on understanding, using and writing English for all 6- to 12-year olds.

Better English, Introductory Book and Books 1-5: a complete English course from about 6-12 years; illustrated in colour.

English Workbooks, Books 1-8: a graded course in punctuation, spelling, vocabulary, comprehension and composition. The first two are intended for infants.

English Workbooks for the Caribbean, Books 1-8: a workbook course specially written for primary schools in the Caribbean; also suitable for immigrants; illustrated in colour.

Structural English Workbooks, Books 1-8: a carefully graded workbook course teaching English as a foreign language to primary schools in West Africa.

English Now, Books 1-5: a complete course in magazine form for the less academic secondary pupil; illustrated in colour.

© RONALD RIDOUT 1960
Eighth impression 1975   3.57511
ISBN 0 602 20992 7   Product No. 028594800
Published by Ginn & Co Ltd, Elsinore House,
Buckingham Street, Aylesbury, Bucks   HP20 2NQ
PRINTED IN GREAT BRITAIN BY R. & R. CLARK LTD, EDINBURGH

PREFACE

THERE are many good reference books on the spelling, use and history of words, but they are geared to the needs of the advanced student, and few, if any, of them are suitable for the average pupil at school or for the foreigner who is still learning the language. In *All about English Words* I have therefore devised a book that will cater for the needs of those who, young or old, require a reference book that is at once comprehensive and yet easily handled. While keeping it free from the niceties of mere erudition, I have made it as complete as possible.

The range of *All about English Words* does, I hope, justify its title. All that is worth saying about English spelling has been included : to have said any more would, at this level, merely confuse. Words have been looked at from many different points of view : to have looked at them from more subtle points of view would have been irrelevant to the needs and capacities of the wide public envisaged. They have been looked at from the points of view of their pronunciation, grammatical function, literal meaning, figurative meaning, build-up, history, derivation, special use and even abuse. In the process, a great deal of useful everyday information about words has been supplied and tabulated. The key to this detailed information is of course the Index, of which it is assumed that the teacher and the student alike will make the fullest use.

Those who have been using the *Word Perfect* series will readily appreciate that this reference book is the natural conclusion to the series. In the earlier books we gradually covered the various aspects of words by a steady accumulation, whilst deliberately avoiding too much systematizing, on the grounds that it was practice rather than theory that was required. It logically follows that the final book should bring under one cover all that has been done, and arrange it in a systematic but simplified way, filling in any gaps that remained. *All about English Words* is therefore the last book of *Word Perfect*, and I hope that it will not only serve as such but will have the added value of a complete reference book that the pupil will be able to use during the last year or two at school, and will wish to take with him into the adult world when he leaves.

As I say, however, in "To the User of this Book" on page vi, *All about English Words* is a practice book as well as a reference book. Exercises follow each aspect of the subject. They are not casually added to test the grasp of what has been read. They are meant to teach, and will in fact do so every bit as much as the main text. We all learn by practice. But to be entirely effective, it must be correct practice. So I have whenever possible continued the self-help method of the earlier books to ensure that the exercises will produce correct answers and therefore correct practice. In this way the exercises are self-teaching and an essential feature of the book.

HASLEMERE, 1960   R. R.

CONTENTS

TO THE USER OF THIS BOOK

I have in earlier books explained the self-help method by which I have tried to help you to help yourself to get the best out of *Word Perfect*. In *All about English Words*, which is the last of the series, my aim and method have been the same, except that I have tried to do something more : I have gathered up all the points we have dealt with and set them down, along with any missing ones, to make a complete account. In this way the last book becomes a reference book as well as a practice book.

It has, therefore, two quite different functions. It can, on the one hand, be used to refer to when you want to look something up ; and we have added an index for this purpose. On the other hand, it can be used as a book to work steadily through. But whichever way it is in fact used, may I suggest that you always do the relevant practice ? We do not learn a thing merely by reading about it ; we learn by doing it. And we learn best by doing it correctly—an outcome I have tried to guarantee by the self-help method.

RONALD RIDOUT

SPELLING RULES and PATTERNS

1

e t s x
u i y r

SPELLING RULES AND PATTERNS

Most of the difficulties of English spelling arise from the fact that words are spelt according to their historical form rather than their sound. To put it another way, English spelling is etymological rather than phonetic. Thus the word *rough* is spelt as it is because in Old English it was pronounced with a guttural sound represented by *gh*, though today it is pronounced as if it were spelt *ruff*.

In earlier times spelling was much more phonetic than it is today. Chaucer, Shakespeare and Milton, for example, were all sensible enough to let the spelling as far as possible represent the sound. But during the eighteenth century the pedants came along and fixed the spelling according to what they considered to be sound etymology. Even so, they made mistakes which have been perpetuated. For instance, Dr Johnson in his Dictionary spelt the Old English verb *ake* with a *ch* (*ache*), as if it came from the Greek. This has given us an odd spelling that has not even the justification of etymology for its oddness.

Since spellings were finally fixed, pronunciation has changed considerably; so that today our spellings are so remote from their pronunciation that if English is to become a real international language, some reform of its spelling will be essential.

In the meantime we must take our spelling as we find it and try to render the bugbear as harmless as possible. Indeed, if we make ourselves familiar with certain rules and patterns, we can account for over 80 per cent of all English words. This has been the purpose of *Word Perfect*. Were no such guidance available, it would not have been possible to teach spelling, and so a spelling course would be out of the question. We should have had to learn every word separately.

In previous books we have covered practically all those rules and patterns. We begin this last book by gathering them together for revision. Then we shall go on to consider special groups of words for their meaning, usage, pronunciation, history and derivation, and other points of interest.

RULE I

One of the simplest rules states that when the sound is like *ee* in *meet*, we use *i* before *e* except after *c*. The only exceptions to this rule are *seize, weird, counterfeit*. Words like *fancied* and *agencies* are not real exceptions since they follow Rule II.

RULE II

Words ending in *–y* preceded by a consonant change the *y* into *i* before any suffix except *–ing*, e.g. *try–tries–tried–trier*, but *trying*; *marry–marries–married–marriage*, but *marrying*; *busy–business–busier–busiest*, but *busying*; *study–studies–studied–studious*, but *studying*. Exceptions are : *shyness–shyly, dryness* (but usually *drily*), *slyness–slyly*.

RULE III

Words ending in *–y* preceded by a vowel retain the *–y* before any suffix, e.g. *employ–employs–employed–employer–employee–employing*. There are a few common exceptions: *lay–layer–laying*, but *laid*; *say–sayer–saying*, but *said*. Similarly: *pay*, but *paid–repaid*; *day–days*, but *daily*; *gay–gayer*, but *gaily*.

RULE IV

In words of one syllable that end in a single consonant preceded by a single vowel, you double the consonant when you add a suffix beginning with a vowel (*beg–begging–beggar, slip–slipper–slippery*). This means, of course, that you do not double the consonant if the word ends in two consonants (*butt–butted, fast–fasted*), or if it has a double vowel (*feel–feeling–feeler, brief–briefer—briefly*), or if the suffix begins with a consonant, e.g. *plan–planning–planner*, but *planless*; *fit–fitter–fittest–fitting–fitted*, but *fitful–fitness*; *star–starred–starring*, but *starless–starlet*. The exceptions are: *bus–buses, gas–gases, wool–woollen*.

RULE V

In words of more than one syllable ending in a single consonant preceded by a single vowel, you double the final consonant only if the last syllable is stressed (*debit–debited*, but *omit–omitted*). As in Rule IV, you do not double the consonant if it is preceded by a double vowel (*despair–despaired*) or another consonant (*depart–departed*), or if it is followed by a suffix beginning with a consonant (*quarrel–quarrelled*, but *quarrelsome*).

The most numerous exceptions to this rule are words ending in *–l*. These usually double the *l* even when the accent does not fall on the last syllable, e.g. *travel–traveller–travelling–travelled*; *counsel – counsellor – counselling – counselled*. But note *parallel–paralleled, civil–civility*.

Other exceptions are: *worship–worshipping–worshipped, outfit–outfitter, kidnap–kidnapped*.

Certain words appear to be exceptions though they are not, e.g. *preference, deference*. The stem verb is accented on the last syllable: *pre-fer', de-fer'*; but in the noun the accent is shifted to the first syllable: *pref'-er-ence, def'-er-ence*.

Rule VI

A very minor rule is that when adverbs in –*ly* are formed from words ending in –*l* or –*ll*, the ending should always be –*lly*, e.g. *full–fully, beautiful–beautifully, level–levelly, shrill–shrilly.*

Rule VII

Words ending in a single *e* (or mute *e*, as it is usually called) drop the *e* when adding a suffix beginning with a vowel, and retain it when adding a suffix beginning with a consonant, e.g. *love–loving–lovable*, but *lovely* ; *bore–boring–bored*, but *boredom* ; *sterile–sterility–sterilize*, but *sterilely* ; *bereave–bereaved–bereaving*, but *bereavement*.

A fairly large group of exceptions consists of those words ending in –*ce* or –*ge*, since these retain the *e* before –*ous* and –*ble* in order to keep the *s* and *j* (dʒ) sounds, e.g. *notice–noticeable, courage–courageous, gauge–gaugeable.*

Other exceptions are : *awe–awful, judge–judgment, true–truly, due–duly, acknowledge–acknowledgment, shoe–shoeing, hoe–hoeing, toe–toeing, singe–singeing* (to distinguish it from *singing*), *dye–dyeing* (to distinguish it from *dying*), *argue–argument, acre–acreage, glue–gluey, whole–wholly.*

Rule VIII

Notice ; *gentle–gently, able–ably, notable–notably.* These look like exceptions to Rule VII. In fact they are a rule to themselves : all words ending in –*le* drop the –*le* when adding –*ly* to form the adverb. If this were not so, we should have such ungainly spellings as *ablely, gentlely* ; and of course we do not pronounce them like that.

Rule IX

Etymologically (i.e. according to the history of the word) we ought to use the suffix –*ize* in spelling all those words that derive from the Greek –*izo*. The suffix can convey such meanings as *to make*, *to become*, *to use*, *to act like* (or *as*), and has the further advantage of being phonetic and therefore showing the pronunciation at a glance. According to this rule, the following should be spelt with –*ise*, since they do not derive from the Greek and the suffix does not denote any of the meanings mentioned above:

advertise	compromise	excise	merchandise
advise	demise	exercise	premise
apprise	despise	franchise	revise
chastise	devise	guise	supervise
circumcise	disguise	improvise	surmise
comprise	enterprise	incise	surprise

All the other words ending in the same sound should be spelt with –*ize*, e.g. *legalize* (to make legal), *fossilize* (to become a fossil), *economize* (to use economy), *tyrannize* (to act like or as a tyrant). On the other hand there is a growing tendency to spell all these words with –*ise*, just as the French spell them with –*iser*, e.g. *légaliser*, *fossiliser*, *économiser*, *tyranniser*, and it is not now considered incorrect to use –*ise*. In fact, G. H. Vallins, in *Good English: How to Write It*, goes so far as to say:

"Pedants and printers keep alive a distinction between –*ise* and –*ize* as verb endings. No one knows why. The ordinary man does not care a brass farthing, and uses –*ise* for them all. If those who write for publication would only stick to their guns and defy the tyranny of the influential Printing Houses, they would soon bring about a minor but useful reform. The artificial distinction based on an etymological subtlety that cannot be known to the ordinary man is unnecessary archaism, and ought to be abolished forthwith."

Rule X

The general rule for making the plural of nouns in English is : add *–s* to the singular form. But in adding the *–s* suffix we may influence the spelling of the word. It is convenient to make eight sub-rules :

(a) Nouns ending in the sibilants (hissing sounds) *s*, *sh*, *ch*, *z*, *x* add *–es* to show the phonetic change, e.g. *gas–gases, mass–masses, brush–brushes, watch–watches, buzz–buzzes, box–boxes*.

(b) Nouns ending in a consonant plus *–y* change the *y* into *i* and add *–es*, e.g. *berry–berries, ruby–rubies*. But those ending in a vowel plus *–y* follow the general rule, e.g. *valley–valleys, toy–toys*.

(c) Some nouns ending in *f* or *–fe* follow the general rule ; some change the *f* into *v* and add *–es* (or *–s* in the case of *–fe* words). Here are the main ones :

bailiff–bailiffs	calf–calves
carafe–carafes	elf–elves
chief–chiefs	half–halves
cliff–cliffs	knife–knives
cuff–cuffs	leaf–leaves
dwarf–dwarfs	life–lives
giraffe–giraffes	loaf–loaves
hoof–hoofs	self–selves
plaintiff–plaintiffs	sheaf–sheaves
roof–roofs	shelf–shelves
scarf–scarfs	thief–thieves
turf–turfs	wife–wives
wharf–wharfs	wolf–wolves

The *–ves* list is complete, but there are many more *–fs* words, so the quickest way of dealing with the problem is to memorize those ending in *–ves*, though it must be pointed out that *hoofs*, *scarfs*, *turfs* and *wharfs* are sometimes spelt with *–ves*.

(d) Most of the familiar nouns ending in *–o* add *–es* for the plural, e.g. *hero–heroes, negro–negroes, no–noes, potato–potatoes.* (The main exceptions are *dynamos, magnetos, photos, pianos, stylos,* which are contractions of longer words.) The less familiar words—longer words, rare words, foreign words, proper names—follow the general rule by adding *–s,* e.g. *archipelagos, bravados, cameos, folios, generalissimos, ghettos, infernos, manifestos, Romeos.*

(e) There is a small collection of nouns that have only one form to indicate both singular and plural. They are : *aircraft, cod, deer, forceps, grouse* (bird), *salmon, sheep, swine.*

(f) Then there are those with no singular form, e.g. *alms, eaves, measles, news, riches, tidings* and all the many nouns ending in *–ics,* e.g. *athletics, mathematics, politics.* These plural nouns often take a singular verb, e.g. "The news *is* most encouraging today". We even speak of giving *an* alms. Others are plural nouns taking plural verbs but describing single things, e.g. *bellows, breeches, pants, pincers, pliers, scissors, shears, tongs, trousers.* With these we always imply "a pair of", and "pair" is singular.

(g) Those nouns that depart entirely from *–s* for the plural are either : odd survivors of Old English, e.g. *man–men, woman–women, child–children, brother–brethren, penny–pence, ox–oxen, foot–feet, tooth–teeth, louse–lice, mouse–mice, goose–geese* ; or words borrowed from other languages and retaining their foreign plurals, e.g. *terminus–termini, bureau–bureaux.* Generally speaking, when these become fully absorbed into our language they lose their foreign plural and take an ordinary English plural. Thus the plural of *index* was *indices,* but already we speak of *indexes,* except in mathematics. But if the English plural would be awkward, the foreign plural may continue to be used. Thus it is unlikely that the plural of *crisis* will ever be *crisises,* since *crises* is much easier to say. On the next page is a list of the more common foreign plurals :

addendum–addenda

analysis–analyses

antenna–antennae

appendix–appendices

automaton–automata

axis–axes

basis–bases

criterion–criteria

datum–data

erratum–errata

focus–foci

formula–formulae

fungus–fungi

hypothesis–hypotheses

index–indices

larva–larvae

libretto–libretti

maximum–maxima

memorandum–memoranda

minimum–minima

nebula–nebulae

nucleus–nuclei

oasis–oases

parenthesis–parentheses

phenomenon–phenomena

plateau–plateaux

radius–radii

sanatorium–sanatoria

spectrum–spectra

stimulus–stimuli

stratum–strata

synopsis–synopses

tableau–tableaux

terminus–termini

thesis–theses

tumulus–tumuli

(h) The plural of compound nouns is a minor rule to itself. Most compound nouns consist of adjective plus noun. Thus blackberry = black + berry. At first it was two words. Then it became hyphenated. Now it is one word. Such words form their plurals in the same way as the noun part alone forms it, e.g. *blackberry–blackberries, Frenchman–Frenchmen*. If the adjective, or adjective equivalent, comes after the noun part, the plural ending still has to be added to the noun part and therefore comes in the middle of the compound word, e.g. *courts-martial, fathers-in-law, knights-errant, lookers-on*. Where the singular ending is *–ful*, the plural ending is not added to the noun part but to the suffix, e.g. *basketfuls, cupfuls*. In a few instances, where the parts of the compound are two nouns, both parts take the plural ending, e.g. *menservants, Lords Justices*.

Rule XI

Some spelling books say that the final double *–ll* of a word used
to form a compound becomes a single *l*. This is quite untrue
as a rule, since there are far more exceptions than instances.
Some monosyllabic words do, however, lose an *l* in forming
certain compounds.

all : *almost, alone, already, almighty, altogether, always.* (But *alright*
   is still considered a vulgarism, and *all right* is preferred.)

full : *beautiful, careful, tactful, hopeful* and in all other words
   where *full* is an adjectival suffix. Also in *fulfil* and *fulsome* ;
   but *full-blooded, full-time,* etc.

still : *distil, instil* ; but *standstill.*

till : *until.*

well : *welcome, welfare* ; but *well-being, well-nigh,* etc. and
   farewell, speedwell.

There are dozens that keep the double *ll*, e.g. *nightfall,*
pitfall, waterfall, snowball, recall, install, pell-mell, mis-spell, retell,
foretell, undersell, windmill, kill-joy, allspice, all-knowing.

Rule XII

The *–y* we add to make an adjective may be regarded as a
vowel. We therefore drop the *e* mute according to Rule VI,
e.g. *louse–lousy, nose–nosy, plague–plaguy.* But notice *blue–bluey,*
glue–gluey. Notice also that if the word already ends in *–y*
and we want to add a *–y* we insert an *e* to avoid *–yy*, e.g. *clayey.*

Rule XIII

Do we write *connection* or *connexion*? Its etymology (Lat.
connexio) approves the latter. But as the English verb is spelt
connect and as there are so many more nouns that are spelt
–ction, it is now more usual to use *connection*. The other nouns
that may be spelt with *–xion* or *–ction* are : *deflexion, inflexion* and
reflexion.

Rule XIV

The suffixes *–or*, *–our* are really one and the same. From about A.D. 1300 till the sixteenth century *–our* was usual. Then during the Renaissance it was felt that the suffix should be spelt like the one in Latin, viz. *–or*. But the change was incomplete; some words dropped the *u*, and some retained it. Thus we have *curator, horror, motor, purveyor, senior, squalor, terror, tremor,* but *clamour, colour, honour, humour, odour, paramour, saviour, vapour.* The position is further complicated by the fact that some of the words in *–our* revert to *–or* when adding a suffix, e.g. *honour–honourable,* but *honorary*; *humour–humouring,* but *humorist, humorous*; *vigour,* but *vigorous, invigorate.* Similarly *amorous, clamorous, glamorous, vaporous.*

It would clearly be simpler if, like the Americans, we dropped the *u* from the whole lot.

Rule XV

There is similar confusion about dropping a neutral vowel (a vowel letter pronounced like *e* in unstressed *the*) before a suffix beginning with a vowel. This never happens with the normal *–ed*, *–ing* endings of the participles; but sometimes does with *–ance*, *–ous*, *–ess*, *–y*, *–al*, e.g. *remember–remembering,* but *remembrance*; *enter–entered,* but *entrance, entry*; *monster,* but *monstrous*; *conductor,* but *conductress*; *neuter,* but *neutral.*

The dropping of *o* in certain words is somewhat similar, e.g. *pronounce–pronunciation, denounce–denunciation, renounce–renunciation.*

Rule XVI

The verbs *advise, devise, license, practise, prophesy* all take *c* in the noun form: *some advice, that device, your licence, this practice, a prophecy.*

W.P. BK. VIII—B

Rule XVII

There is no satisfactory rule for the spelling of an adjective ending in *–able* or *–ible*, but here are two useful, though not infallible guides:

(a) If you happen to know Latin you will find that those derived from infinitives ending in *–are* mostly have *–able*, while those deriving from infinitives ending in *–ere* or *–ire* mostly have *–ible*, e.g. *applicable* (*applicare*), *educable* (*educare*), *excitable* (*excitare*), *insuperable* (*superare*), *invulnerable* (*vulnerare*); *accessible* (*accedere*), *comprehensible* (*comprehendere*), *contemptible* (*contemnere*), *divisible* (*dividere*), *fallible* (*fallere*); *audible* (*audire*), *exhaustible* (*exhaurire*).

(b) When you can form a word in the same family ending in *–ation*, the adjective will end in *–able*, e.g.:

durable (duration)	irreparable (reparation)
estimable (estimation)	perturbable (perturbation)
execrable (execration)	quotable (quotation)
illimitable (limitation)	reputable (reputation)
inviolable (violation)	venerable (veneration)

When you can form a word ending in *–ion*, *–tion*, *–ive* only, the adjective will usually end in *–ible*, e.g.:

audible (audition)	digestible (digestive)
combustible (combustion)	irrepressible (repressive)
convertible (conversion)	perceptible (perception)
defensible (defensive)	reversible (reversion)

Here are some more useful *–able –ible* adjectives:

affable	indubitable	compatible	flexible
attributable	inscrutable	deducible	incorrigible
enforceable	remediable	discernible	invincible
equitable	venerable	expressible	tangible

Rule XVIII

For the sake of euphony (ease of pronunciation), the longer words ending in –ate drop the –ate before adding –able, e.g. *appreciate–appreciable*, *calculate–calculable*, *estimate–estimable*, *navigate–navigable*.

Rule XIX

Grammatically speaking, English words do not have genders. Unlike the French, we do not have to remember that *book* is masculine, while *pen* is feminine. We do, however, make changes in a limited number of words according to the sex of the creature named. There are four types of change :

(a) We modify the masculine name, e.g. *man–woman*, or the feminine name, e.g. *bride–bridegroom, widow–widower*.

(b) We add a suffix, e.g. *actor–actress, god–goddess, mayor–mayoress, negro–negress, sultan–sultana*.

(c) We alter part of a compound, e.g. *billy-goat–nanny-goat, landlord–landlady, manservant–maidservant*.

(d) We use an entirely different word, e.g. *son–daughter*.

Here is a list for reference. The male names are placed first.

abbot	abbess	executor	executrix	monk	nun
bachelor	spinster	fox	vixen	nephew	niece
baron	baroness	gander	goose	peacock	peahen
beau	belle	hart	hind	ram	ewe
boar	sow	heir	heiress	sir	madam
brave	squaw	hero	heroine	sire	dam
buck	doe	host	hostess	stag	hind
colt	filly	husband	wife	stallion	mare
dog	bitch	lad	lass	steer	heifer
drake	duck	lord	lady	testator	testatrix
duke	duchess	marquis	marchioness	waiter	waitress
earl	countess	masseur	masseuse	widower	widow
emperor	empress	master	mistress	wizard	witch

Rule XX

The endings *-us* and *-ous* are pronounced alike. A useful little rule to note is that the nouns end in *-us*, while the adjectives end in *-ous*, e.g. nouns : *fungus, genus, humus, mucus, phosphorus* ; adjectives : *anonymous, callous, famous, mucous.*

Rule XXI

Verbs ending in *c*, like *bivouac, frolic, mimic, panic, picnic, traffic*, add a *k* before *-ed, -y, -ing, -er* to keep the *c* hard in sound, e.g. *bivouac–bivouacking, frolic–frolicsome–frolicking, mimic–mimicked, panic–panicking–panicky, picnic–picnicking–picknicker.*

Rule XXII

How can we tell whether a word should begin with *for–* or *fore–*, since they are pronounced alike ? It is not difficult if we remember that *fore–* always has to do with the idea of priority in time, position or rank, e.g. *forejudge, foreland, foreman.* (The only exception is *foreclose*, which does not derive from the Old English *fore*, but from the Latin *foris*, meaning *outside*.) The prefix *for–*, on the other hand, has a variety of meanings. It was once very common, but now survives only in *forbear, forbid, forby, fordo, forfeit, forfend, forgather, forget, forgive, forgo, forlorn, forsake, forsooth, forspent, forswear, forworn.* Notice that *forgo* means *to go without*, while *forego* means *to go before.*

Rule XXIII

Is the second vowel in *narrative* pronounced as *i, e, u* or *a* ? Its sound is what we call a neutral vowel (phonetic symbol ə) and gives no clue to the spelling. But if we know a related word where the neutral vowel is accented—in this case *narrate*—we shall be in no doubt about the spelling. Other examples are : relative (relate)   democracy (democratic)   definite (definition) sedative (sedate)   apology (apologetic)   author (authority)

Rule XXIV

One of the most helpful guides to correct spelling and meaning is obtained from understanding how words are built up from their component parts. The central brick, which tells you what family the word belongs to, is called the root or stem. The brick that goes before it is called a prefix, and the one that comes after it is a suffix. Words may be built up in the following patterns: (a) the root alone; (b) prefix+root; (c) root +suffix; (d) prefix+root+suffix. Thus:

(a)	do	man	port	stamp
(b)	over–do	un–man	trans–port	re–stamp
(c)	do–ing	man–ly	port–able	stamp–ed
(d)	over–do–ing	un–man–ly	trans–port–able	re–stamp–ed

The root may not, of course, be a recognizable word, but a French, Latin or Greek root. Thus the root in *conscious* is the Latin root *sci* that appears in *scio* (I know). The word is therefore built up like this: *con–sci–ous*.

Sometimes the pattern is complicated by there being more than one prefix or suffix. The word *unconsciously*, for example, has two prefixes and two suffixes, and is built up like this: *un–con–sci–ous–ly*.

Knowing how a word is built up is a vital guide to meaning. For instance, if we know that *describe, inscribe* and *subscribe* are made up of the Latin root *scribo* (I write) plus the prefix *de–*, *in–* and *sub–* respectively, we automatically know that *describe* means to write about, *inscribe* to write in and *subscribe* to write under and so show agreement.

It also helps us to know the correct spelling. For example, if we know that *cafeteria* (the first *e* of which is not accented and therefore neutral) is made up of *café*+*teria*, we can be sure that the fourth letter of *cafeteria* will be *e*. Similarly if we know that *iridescent* comes from *iris +escent*, we can be sure that the third letter of *iridescent* will be *i*.

It is particularly helpful in spelling words with double consonants at the end of the prefix. Thus if we know how the following words are made up, there will be no risk of our putting a double consonant for a single one and *vice versa*:

connect	con+nect	interrupt	inter+rupt
disappear	dis+appear	interrogate	inter+rogate
dissolve	dis+solve	intervene	inter+vene
miscalculate	mis+calculate	unnerve	un+nerve
innocent	in+nocent	professor	pro+fessor
inoculate	in+oculate	suppress	sup+press

RULE XXV

The reason for a double consonant is sometimes obscured by assimilation. This term is applied to the process by which the last consonant of the prefix is made like the first consonant of the root. Thus the word *immobile* is made up of *in +mobile* (*mobilis*), and so we have a double *m*. Similarly the word *assimilation* has a double *s* because it is made up of *ad +similis* (like to) and the *d* of *ad* has been assimilated by the *s* of *similis*. Here are some more examples of double consonants produced by assimilation:

ad +cumulo (I make into a heap) =accumulate
ad +ficio (I connect one thing with another) =affect
ad +gressio (a step or pace towards) =aggression
ad +nihilo (I bring to nothing) =annihilate
ad +plaudo (I clap with my hands) =applaud
ad +socio (I join or unite with) =associate
com +ligo (I tie or bind together) =college
com +respondeo (I respond with) =correspond
com +laboro (I work with) =collaborate

dis +fero (I carry in different ways) = differ
dis +fidens (not bold or trusting) = diffident
in +legibilis (that cannot be read) = illegible
in +mineo (I hang over or threaten) = imminent
in +modestus (not modest) = immodest
in +religiosus (not religious) = irreligious
ob +fendo (I dash or strike against) = offend
ob +pressio (a pressing down) = oppression
sub +cumbo (I lie down under) = succumb
sub +pleo (I fill up from the bottom) = supply

RULE XXVI

There are four main ways of forming opposites or antonyms in English.

(a) We can add a prefix. Thus the opposite of *visible* is *invisible* and the opposite of *obedient* is *disobedient*. *dis–, il–, im–, in–, ir–, mis–, non–, un–* are the main prefixes used.

creditable–discreditable
reputable–disreputable
legitimate–illegitimate
material–immaterial
perturbable–imperturbable
civility–incivility
opportune–inopportune
religious–irreligious

fortune–misfortune
trust–mistrust
conformist–nonconformist
entity–nonentity
sense–nonsense
congenial–uncongenial
expurgated–unexpurgated
obtrusive–unobtrusive

For doubling the *l* in *illegitimate*, the *m* in *immaterial* and the *r* in *irreligious*, see Rule XXV. Also note that *in* becomes *im* before *p*, e.g. *impartial*.

(b) Sometimes we can change the prefix. Thus *external* is the opposite of *internal*, and *emigrant* the opposite of *immigrant*. Some others are: *ascend–descend, encourage–discourage, export–import, extensive–intensive, increase–decrease, introvert–extrovert.*

(c) With some adjectives we can change the suffix, e.g.: *harmful–harmless, merciful–merciless, purposeful–purposeless, tasteful–tasteless.*

(d) In the majority of cases we must look for an entirely different word, e.g. *ancient–modern, harmony–discord, innocently–guiltily, occupy–vacate.*

Any one word may have more than one antonym. This is because the exact meaning of a word depends upon how it is used—upon its context. The antonym we should choose in any particular case therefore depends upon the context in which it is to be used. For example, the opposite of a soft voice is a loud voice, yet the opposite of a soft bed would be a hard bed, and the opposite of a soft character might be a strong character.

EXERCISES

On Rule I

A. Can you write this out from memory or dictation without making any spelling mistakes?

> So weird and white and great in height,
> The monster is an eerie sight
>   Perceived in moonlight's brief emission.
> With grievous qualms I seek retreat
> From this vast ghastly counterfeit
>   Of some fierce ghostly apparition,
> But piercing breezes on me seize
> And set me quaking at the knees—
>   A quite disquieting position.
> Besieged by doubts my valour fails.
> I crouch till welcome dawn unveils
>   A snowman for my recognition!

CLIFFORD WITTING

B. Arrange each of these groups in alphabetical order:
  1. niece, relief, conceit, perceive, pier, siege, ceiling
  2. deceive, seize, believable, conceive, receive, besiege

On Rule II

Add *–es, –ed, –ing* to each of these verbs:
1. reply	3. embody	5. fancy	7. lobby
2. defy	4. modify	6. prophesy	8. levy

On Rule III

A. From what base word has each of these been formed by adding a suffix?
1. valleys	3. hurrying	5. repayment	7. gaily
2. penniless	4. carriage	6. defiant	8. batteries

B. Add *–er*, *–est*, *–ly* to each of these adjectives :

1. podgy	3. cushy	5. stuffy	7. coy
2. healthy	4. greedy	6. grumpy	8. gay

C. Make new words by adding one of these suffixes to each of those below : *–ment*, *–ies*, *–some*, *–ly*, *–ness*, *–age*, *–er*, *–ous*, *–ful*, *–ish*, *–less*, *–able*. Use each suffix once only.

1. weary	4. deploy	7. democracy	10. vary
2. boy	5. lonely	8. remedy	11. day
3. duty	6. marry	9. betray	12. melody

On Rule IV

Arrange each of these lists in alphabetical order :

1. shopper, shipment, slippery, sloppy, slopped, sluttish
2. cutter, capped, capless, clapper, chummy, charred
3. bidder, biddable, baggy, bagful, biggest, bigness, blurred

On Rule V

A. Divide 1-4 of the following into three syllables each, and 5-8 into four syllables each, and show where the accent falls :

1. filleted	5. benefited
2. beginning	6. intermittent
3. reference	7. uncommitted
4. committee	8. preferable

B. Which word is out of place in each of these lists ?
1. equipped, preferred, controlled, committee, committed
2. tonnage, stoppage, occurrence, recurrence, deferred, acquittal
3. deterrent, different, instalment, recurrent, intermittent

C. Add *–ing* and *–ed* to each of these verbs :

1. befit	3. defer	5. gossip	7. gallop
2. benefit	4. differ	6. prefer	8. rebut

D. Explain why these words did or did not double the final consonant of the stem when the suffix was added. There are no exceptions in the list.

1. slotted   3. forgetting   5. rebuttal   7. redeeming
2. fitment   4. submitted   6. demanding 8. biased

E. Pick out the seven words that obey Rule V, and the five that are exceptions to it :

1. focused   4. quarrelled   7. propeller 10. panelling
2. limited   5. worshipped   8. forgotten 11. paralleled
3. galloper   6. gossiper   9. atlases   12. walloping

F. Make new words by adding –er and –ed to each of these :

1. transmit 3. demur   5. abet   7. control 9. worship
2. support   4. transfer 6. drum   8. develop 10. quiz

ON RULE VI

Make adverbs ending in –ly from these adjectives :

1. wilful   2. awful   3. full   4. shrill   5. cool

ON RULE VII

A. From what stem words ending in mute *e* do these come ?

1. monotonous 3. pleasant   5. servant   7. delegation
2. futility   4. grievance 6. sincerity 8. fortunate

B. Make new words by adding –ous to each of these :

1. fame   3. outrage   5. ridicule   7. advantage
2. desire   4. monotone   6. pore   8. gelatine

C. Pick out the seven words that obey Rule VII, and the five that are exceptions to it :

1. truly   5. duly   9. guileless
2. guidance   6. endurance   10. dispensable
3. insurance   7. serviceable 11. disadvantageous
4. arguable   8. judgment   12. reversible

D. Make new words by adding the suffix indicated to each of the following stems :

1. grieve (–ance)	6. awe (–fully)	11. argue (–ment)
2. store (–age)	7. courage (–ous)	12. argue (–able)
3. true (–ly)	8. survive (–al)	13. relegate (–ed)
4. singe (–ed)	9. please (–ure)	14. immediate (–ly)
5. whole (–ly)	10. glue (–y)	15. exquisite (–ness)

E. Make a single alphabetical list of these words :

parachuting	traceable	changeable	rhymeless
dyeing	separately	vagueness	rhyming
replaceable	receding	inconceivable	favouritism

On Rule VIII

Make adverbs by adding –*ly* to these adjectives :

1. simple	3. subtle	5. inseparable	7. insoluble
2. ample	4. whole	6. justifiable	8. invisible

On Rule IX

A. Which words on page 6 have the following meanings ? If you do your exercise correctly your word list will be in alphabetical order.

1. to inform or make aware of
2. to punish or beat
3. to include or consist of
4. to settle something by mutual consent
5. to transfer property by will or lease (legal term)
6. to cut out a passage of a book or part of the body
7. citizen's right to vote at elections
8. to make up on the spot without preparation
9. to make a cut in ; engrave
10. commodities ; goods offered for sale
11. to say or write by way of introduction
12. to suspect the existence of ; make a guess

B. Write definitions of the following verbs :
1. anglicize   3. rationalize   5. fossilize   7. monopolize
2. jeopardize   4. immobilize   6. idealize   8. devitalize

C. Write each of these lists in alphabetical order :
1. generalize, apologize, specialize, socialize, sympathize
2. vocalize, tantalize, acclimatize, vaporize, antagonize, authorize
3. mesmerize, militarize, memorize, magnetize, minimize
4. idolize, itemize, internationalize, immobilize, neutralize, naturalize, nationalize, particularize

D. Abstract nouns ending in *–ation* are formed from these verbs according to Rule VII.   Form such nouns :
1. nationalize   3. organize   5. mobilize   7. mechanize
2. modernize   4. civilize   6. equalize   8. fraternize

E. Prepare for dictation the quotation from G. H. Vallins on page 6.

ON RULE X

A. Give the singular of these nouns :
1. inquiries   4. tomatoes   7. gratuities   10. anchovies
2. policies   5. sheaves   8. housewives   11. biographies
3. impurities   6. monkeys   9. successes   12. authorities

B. Make a single alphabetical list of these nouns :
territories   sundries   ceremonies   shrubberies   irrelevancies
decencies   trophies   tyrannies   wallabies   thingummies

C. Give the plural form of these nouns :
1. galley   4. agency   7. dinghy   10. autobiography
2. variety   5. valley   8. prophecy   11. deficiency
3. activity   6. sheaf   9. symphony   12. absurdity

D. Place these plural nouns with their definitions below. If you do this correctly your list will be in alphabetical order.

fallacies   subsidiaries   minorities   faculties   priorities
auguries   discrepancies   gallantries   dowries   wharfs

1. divinations from the actions of birds
2. lacks of consistency; disagreements
3. money, etc. brought by women to their husbands on marriage
4. mental powers
5. misleading arguments; errors; delusions
6. acts of great courage
7. smaller numbers or parts
8. things coming first in order of importance
9. things or persons that assist or supplement
10. landing-places for cargoes

E. Can you complete these alphabetical series?
1. ambushes, bitches, crutches, ditches, expresses . . .
2. authorities, berries, crannies, deputies, embassies . . .

F. Which of the words mentioned under Rule X (d) have the following meanings? If correct, your list will be in alphabetical order.
1. seas with many islands
2. precious stone carved so that there is a raised part on a coloured background
3. large sheets of paper, each making four pages when folded once
4. parts of cities where Jews were required to live
5. hell-like places
6. electric generators using magnets
7. public declarations making known the motives of one's actions

G. Pick out the word that does not belong to the group:
  1. tongs, pliers, scissors, trousers, pincers
  2. deer, sheep, cod, salmon, aircraft, swine, grouse
  3. measles, mumps, influenza, forceps, bronchitis
  4. trousers, breeches, stockings, eaves, frock-coat
  5. ghettos, alms, pincers, dynamo, billows, riches
  6. politics, news, pianos, physics, riches, pliers, alms

H. Give the plural form of these nouns:
  1. hero   3. deer   5. crescendo   7. aircraft
  2. tomato   4. forceps   6. Nero   8. archipelago

I. Arrange each group in alphabetical order:
  1. theses, synopses, axes, analyses, parentheses, hypotheses
  2. tableaux, plateaux, beaux, bureaux, chateaux
  3. minima, maxima, memoranda, strata, spectra, data
  4. lice, louse, libretti, larvae, pennies, pence, oxen, oases,
     tumuli, teeth, termini, tooth, theses

J. Use the following nouns to complete the sentences below:
strata, nuclei, criteria, antennae, data.

  1. The selection committee applied several different —
for judging the candidates, to ensure that the best in every way
was picked out.
  2. Quite small collections of books and antiquities formed
the — of what are now the Public Library and the Municipal
Museum.
  3. The scientists decided that the — available were insuffi-
cient for any exact conclusion to be reached.
  4. Between the upper and lower — was a layer of rock.
  5. — are the sensory organs found in pairs on the heads
of insects and crustacea.

K. Give the singular form of these plural nouns :

1. fungi   4. axes   7. appendices   10. antennae
2. loci   5. crises   8. indices   11. formulae
3. oxen   6. oases   9. lice   12. larvae

L. Place the right noun from the list on page 9 in front of each definition.   If correct, your list will be in alphabetical order.

1. something to be added
2. the feelers of an insect ; radio aerials
3. the standard by which anything is judged
4. facts from which conclusions can be drawn
5. an error in printing or writing
6. the book or words of an opera or long musical work
7. a cloudy patch of light in the sky produced by groups of many stars
8. the marks (   ) to show an insertion in a sentence
9. the colours of a ray of light separated by a prism
10. a bed or layer of earth, stone, coal, etc.
11. an outline or summary of a book, etc.
12. a mound of earth over a grave

M. Form the plural of these nouns according to Rule X (h) :

1. spoonful   4. Scotsman   7. maid-in-waiting
2. tintack   5. governor-general   8. man-of-war
3. semiquaver   6. Knight Templar   9. coat-of-mail

ON RULE XI

Complete these compound words with a single or double *l* :

1. fu–some   3. disti–   5. a–one   7. we–fare
2. mis-spe–   4. standsti–   6. insta–   8. farewe–

On Rule XII

Make adjectives ending in –*y* from these words :

1. noise	3. choose	5. sky	7. sunshine
2. spike	4. scale	6. glue	8. clique

On Rule XIII

A. Here are sixteen –*ect* verbs that always form their abstract nouns in –*ection*. Form them.

1. reject	6. intersect	12. resurrect
2. recollect	7. inject	13. misdirect
3. bisect	8. disinfect	14. eject
4. vivisect	9. dissect	15. interject
5. project	10. disaffect	16. introspect
	11. affect	

B. Now place each word from A with its definition below. If correct, your list will be in alphabetical order.

1. to have an effect on
2. to divide into two parts
3. to alienate or diminish the affection of
4. to cleanse of infection
5. to cut in pieces
6. to throw out
7. to drive or force into
8. to throw in ; to interpose a remark during conversation
9. to cross each other, as of lines or streets
10. to examine one's own thoughts and feelings
11. to direct wrongly
12. to cast or throw ; to protrude
13. to remember
14. to throw back ; to refuse to receive
15. to revive practice or memory of
16. to dissect living animals

ON RULE XIV

A. *Invigorate* comes from the stem *vigour*. From what stem words do the following come?

1. clamorous 3. humorist 5. discoloration 7. honorary
2. vaporize   4. glamorous 6. odorous   8. evaporate

B. Arrange these words in one alphabetical list:

censor	incisor	aggressor	donor	liquidator
divisor	sponsor	assessor	debtor	instigator
juror	senator	adjudicator	suitor	invigorator
visor	mentor	innovator	ejector	testator

C. Pick out the words in B that have the following meanings. If correct, your list will be in alphabetical order.

1. one who sits as a judge; an arbitrator or umpire
2. the man with the blue pencil
3. one who gives
4. person or thing that expels or throws out
5. one of your front teeth
6. one who brings in something new
7. one who urges on, especially to evil
8. anything that puts new life into
9. wise and faithful counsellor
10. one who makes a will

ON RULE XV

From what stem words have these been formed?

1. ancestry
2. cloistral
3. hindrance
4. encumbrance
5. mispronunciation
6. idolatrous
7. proprietress
8. ambidextrous
9. renunciation
10. benefactress
11. carpentry
12. impropriety

On Rule XVI

Insert the missing *s* or *c* in this sentence:

"I advi–e you not to make a practi–e of prophe–ying unless you have a licen–e to do so."

On Rule XVII

A. The words missing in the following sentences will all be found on page 12.

1. It would be only a slight exaggeration to say that a millionaire is a man of almost — means.
2. This team seems —, since they have never lost a match.
3. Mr Smith's purchases were always of high quality because he dealt only with — traders.
4. Only the outline of the building was — against the night sky, but he was sure that this was the right house.
5. He showed — taste by attending the funeral in a flashy necktie.
6. Although the theft of the necklace was — to the jackdaw, there was no — evidence of this.
7. They decided that the most — arrangement was to divide the money evenly between them.
8. Pierre's reply was given in such rapid French that it was — to the English boy.

B. How could you tell from Rule XVII (b) that each of these should have the ending it has?

1. irritable	5. admissible
2. destructible	6. visible
3. lamentable	7. demonstrable
4. expressible	8. transportable

C. Make adjectives ending in *–able* or *–ible* from these verbs:

1. pronounce	3. reduce	5. refute	7. avert
2. retrieve	4. collapse	6. certify	8. permit

D. Now use the following words in sentences of your own :

1. edible   3. charitable   5. imperceptible
2. debatable   4. incurable   6. imperturbable

On Rule XVIII

A. Form adjectives ending in *–able* from these verbs :

1. separate   4. irritate   7. demonstrate   10. irrigate
2. tolerate   5. imitate   8. negotiate   11. appreciate
3. educate   6. venerate   9. mitigate   12. communicate

B. Put these words with their definitions. Your list, if correct, will be in the reverse of alphabetical order.

inviolable	intolerable	negotiable	incalculable
inseparable	mitigable	permeable	inimitable
venerable	explicable	implacable	ineradicable
appreciable	ineducable	interminable	inalienable

1. worthy of reverence or honour
2. yielding passage to fluids
3. capable of being arranged
4. capable of being alleviated
5. that cannot be violated or injured
6. too much to be endured ; unbearable
7. endless ; tediously lengthy
8. always together
9. matchless ; not to be copied or equalled
10. that cannot be got rid of
11. incapable of being taught anything
12. too numerous to be counted ; beyond reckoning
13. from which one cannot be diverted
14. relentless ; not to be appeased
15. capable of being explained
16. sufficient to be estimated

On Rule XIX

A. Give the correct single word for :

1. a male goose
2. a female fox
3. a male cat
4. an earl's wife
5. a sultan's wife
6. the sister of a person's nephew
7. a woman who receives guests
8. a woman who executes a will
9. a young cow that hasn't had a calf
10. a woman who dies leaving a will

B. Give the noun to name these when of the male sex :

1. a duck
2. a Red Indian
3. a pig
4. a horse
5. a servant
6. a sheep
7. a baby horse
8. a cat

On Rule XX

Define these adjectives, and then use each to complete one of the sentences below : *bulbous, dubious, gibbous, querulous, raucous, viscous.*

1. "Why must it always rain on Saturdays?" asked Jack in a — tone.
2. When the teacher congratulated Tommy on not being bottom of the class, Tommy regarded it as a — compliment.
3. A knobkerrie is a short club with a — head.
4. The poor chaffinch got stuck to the — bird-lime spread on the twigs of the tree.
5. The costermonger's harsh voice sounded more — than ever when I next passed his barrow.
6. The — moon had not yet reached its full.

On Rule XXI

Add *–er* and *–ing* to each of these words :

1. picnic
2. frolic
3. entice
4. enforce
5. mimic
6. bivouac
7. menace
8. traffic

On Rule XXII

A. Write definitions of the following words to show that they all derive from *fore-*, meaning "before" :

1. to foretaste
2. a forelock
3. the foreground
4. to forecast
5. the forecastle
6. to forestall

B. Make one alphabetical list of the following :

foremost	foregoing	forehand	forsworn
foremast	foreboding	forlorn	forewarn
forenoon	forswear	forbidden	forsaken

On Rule XXIII

Suggest how we can be sure of the spelling of the neutral vowels (in italics) by giving a related word in which the corresponding vowel is accented and therefore its spelling obvious.

1. arithm*e*tic   2. hypocr*i*sy   3. friv*o*lous   4. conserv*a*tive

On Rule XXIV

A. Break up the following words into their component parts to show that they are built in the way indicated.

1. *Prefix + root* : dissolve, unwise, prefer, admit, mistake, report, export, deport, import
2. *Root + suffix* : meanly, meanness, meanest, careless, careful, nervous, tidal, courageous
3. *Prefix + root + suffix* : conscience, reporter, department, university, unusual, disestablishment, survival
4. *Two prefixes + root + suffix* : misunderstanding, unconscious, reimporter, indistinctly, superintendent, disinterment
5. *Prefix + root + two suffixes* : unhopefully, repulsiveness, divergently, distastefulness, infamously
6. *Two prefixes + root + two suffixes* : disadvantageousness, uncompromisingly, inconspicuousness, indescribably, inconsistently

B. Break up 1-6 of the following to show that the double consonant is correct, and 7-12 to show that the single consonant is correct :

1. innocently	5. interregnum	9. inimical
2. dissimilar	6. innocuous	10. inexplicable
3. unnatural	7. component	11. misconstrue
4. commit	8. dislocate	12. intervention

C. Define these words and explain how the meaning of each can be arrived at by knowing its component parts :

1. inscribe   3. interrupt   5. remorseless   7. indivisible
2. innocent   4. intervene   6. supersonic   8. exhumation

D. Write each of these lists alphabetically, omitting the misplaced word :

1. discourteous, discernible, dissimilar, disproportionate, disinherited, distemper, disappear
2. miscellaneous, misnomer, misdemeanour, misconception, mischievousness, mis-statement, mishap

On Rule XXV

A. Break up these words into prefix plus root to show how assimilation gives rise to a double consonant. All the prefixes are in the list on page 16, and the following are the roots in alphabetical order : *–curro* (I run), *–facilis* (easy), *–filio* (from *filius*, a son), *–foco* (from *faux*, the throat), *–fusio* (a pouring out), *–legalis* (from *lex*, the law), *–mortalis* (mortal), *–nexio* (a tying, binding), *–pono* (I place), *portunus* (from *portus*, a harbour), *–rogantia* (from *rogo*, I ask), *–rumpo* (I break).

1. illegal	4. annex	7. arrogance	10. oppose
2. immortal	5. succour	8. suffocate	11. opportune
3. diffusion	6. corrupt	9. difficult	12. affiliate

B. Define the following words, and then use them to fill in the gaps in the sentences below :

> assent   acclamation   allusion   collaborate
> annul   opportune   immunity   irrespective

1. Smith and Jones decided to — in writing the book, since Smith was an expert on one aspect and Jones on the other.
2. The speaker's — to the fable of the tortoise and the hare caused some amusement among the audience.
3. The force of the current was sufficient to — all the boy's efforts to row upstream.
4. Vaccination provides — from smallpox.
5. The islanders were saved from starvation by the — arrival of a ship bringing supplies.
6. Membership of the association was open to all, — of race, creed or colour.
7. The news of the half-holiday was received with — by all the children in the class.
8. The farmer would not — to the proposal that an electricity pylon should be erected on his field.

On Rule XXVI

A. Make antonyms for these by adding a prefix to each:

1. gratitude	10. controvertible
2. authentic	11. relevant
3. soluble	12. service
4. legible	13. consequential
5. charitable	14. behave
6. integrate	15. rational
7. moderate	16. consolable
8. appeasable	17. sanitary
9. modest	18. partial

B. Make antonyms from these by changing the prefix or the suffix (in one instance, prefix and suffix) :

1. cheerful   4. forceless   7. inhale   10. incoming
2. ascent   5. enrobe   8. outlet   11. enfranchise
3. exterior   6. upwards   9. careful   12. overstatement

C. Give each of these numbered words its antonym from the numbered list :

1. dissuade   2. furrow   3. bracing   4. douse   5. levity
    enervating   enkindle   persuade   gravity   ridge

D. From the alphabetical list below pick out four antonyms for each of the following :

1. cautious 3. inessential   5. indistinct   7. unsubstantial
2. increase 4. uncongenial 6. civility   8. disreputable

actual, agreeable, clear, congenial, curtail, decrease, diminish, discourtesy, distinct, essential, estimable, favourable, headlong, honest, impoliteness, imprudent, incautious, incivility, indispensable, lessen, necessary, pellucid, rash, real, reputable, respectable, rudeness, solid, substantial, suitable, undimmed, vital

E. Suggest appropriate opposites of these :

1. a hard sum   5. a wild cat   9. a bright light
2. hard luck   6. a wild flower   10. a bright tune
3. a hard winter   7. a wild sea   11. a bright pupil
4. hard water   8. a wild venture   12. a bright colour

You might use : calm, cultivated, dull, easy, good, melancholy, mild, prudent, soft, stupid, subdued, tame

FIRST SPELLING-BEE

Liquids
alcohol
beverage
champagne
cocoa
fluid
lemonade
vinegar
whisky

Flowers
chrysanthemum
daffodil
dahlia
dandelion
geranium
gladiolus
hyacinth
narcissus

Measurements
acre
ampère
calibre
centimetre
fathom
furlong
kilometre
voltage

Food
biscuits
blancmange
carbo-hydrates
dessert
margarine
porridge
proteins
sausages

Hospital
casualty
chloroform
masseur
masseuse
paralysis
sterilize
surgeon
thermometer

Vegetables
asparagus
cabbage
cauliflower
celery
cucumber
lettuce
parsley
rhubarb

Aviation
aerodrome
aeronautics
elevator
fuselage
helicopter
parachute
propeller
Zeppelin

Crime
accomplice
alibi
assassination
counterfeit
delinquent
embezzlement
incendiary
larceny

Traps
accommodation
embarrassment
fulsome
languorous
paraffin
skilful
supersede
tonsillitis

FIRST CHECK ON MEANINGS

Give a single word for each of the following:

1. to give citizens the right to vote (page 35)
2. able to last; resisting wear or decay (12)
3. prejudiced; inclined to one side (21)
4. the feelers of an insect; radio aerials (9)
5. to make up on the spot without preparation (6)
6. a public declaration by some important person or group (8)
7. an error in printing or writing (9)
8. a musical note of half the duration of a quaver (26)
9. the period between the end of one reign and the beginning of the next (33)
10. to foretell future events (19)
11. that cannot be violated or injured (30)
12. well-timed; coming at a favourable moment (33)
13. to alienate or diminish the affection of (27)
14. to free from bacteria or microbes (5)
15. a hell-like place (8)
16. a bed or layer of earth, stone, coal, etc. (9)
17. matchless; not to be copied or equalled (30)
18. protruberant; humped; convex (31)
19. a woman who dies leaving a will (13)
20. a person or thing that expels or throws out (28)
21. deprived of inheritance (33)
22. jelly made from certain parts of an animal by boiling (21)
23. the wife of a marquis (13)
24. bashful; lacking self-confidence (17)
25. to cross each other, as of lines or streets (27)
26. one who urges on, especially to evil (28)
27. a temporary encampment without tents (14)
28. facts from which conclusions can be drawn (9)

29. that can exist together without disagreement (12)
30. a café where the customers fetch their own food from the counter (15)
31. that cannot be got rid of (30)
32. to throw back; to refuse to receive (27)
33. not genuine; made in imitation (3)
34. about to happen any moment (17)
35. tending to soothe (14)
36. incapable of being taught anything (30)
37. to renounce on oath (14)
38. to make less vital; to weaken (23)
39. predictions, originally based on flight of birds (24)
40. a person or thing of no consequence (17)
41. to act like a tyrant (6)
42. a change in the tone or pitch of the voice (10)
43. stopping and beginning again (20)
44. able to use the left hand as well as the right (28)
45. the state of looking dirty, mean and poor (11)
46. a person who brings a lawsuit (7)
47. to encourage, especially in something wrong (21)
48. not able to be doubted (12)
49. electric generators using magnets (8)
50. an attempt to disprove (21)
51. beyond correction (12)
52. brief statements giving a general view (9)
53. to infect mildly with a disease as a safeguard (16)
54. districts inhabited by Jews in cities (8)
55. not able to be repaired (12)
56. something assumed because it seems likely (9)
57. oddments not needing special mention (23)
58. not easily disturbed or confused (17)

PARTS of SPEECH

2

PARTS OF SPEECH

The parts of speech divide words into classes according to their grammatical function in the sentence. As this is not a book about grammar, we are here concerned with the parts of speech mainly from the point of view of meaning. It is necessary first, however, to remind you of the eight different parts of speech and their essential differences.

1. THE NOUN. This names things, creatures, ideas and abstract qualities, e.g. *sugar, lizard, jargon, stickiness*.

2. THE VERB. This says what a person or thing does, is, thinks or suffers, e.g. *waddled, was, ponders, were dissolved*.

3. THE ADJECTIVE. This tells us something about what is named by a noun, e.g. a *valuable* brooch; his *useless* theories.

4. THE ADVERB. This modifies or describes more fully any part of speech except a noun or pronoun, but usually a verb, e.g. sang *boisterously*; *fully* agreed; an *exceedingly* large bun (modifying the adjective).

5. THE PRONOUN. This stands instead of what is named by a noun, e.g. *he, them, ours, none*.

6. THE CONJUNCTION. This is used to join words, phrases or clauses, e.g. bread *and* butter; above the chair *but* under the picture.

7. THE PREPOSITION. This introduces a phrase, e.g. *under* this bed; *in* the morning; *without* any milk.

8. THE INTERJECTION. This represents anything merely exclaimed, e.g. *Oh dear! Damn! Goodness! Hullo!*

The parts of speech are important to any understanding of the use and meaning of words, since a single word may be used as several different parts of speech, and its meaning will naturally vary accordingly, as may be seen from the use of *brown* in the following:

As a noun: Brown is a colour that I dislike intensely.

As a verb: I always brown very quickly at the seaside.

As an adjective: Suddenly they came face to face with a brown bear.

EXERCISES

A. One example of each of the parts of speech has been italicized below. Identify all eight.

1. In the dark woods *we* heard a nightingale singing.
2. The bus did not arrive, *so* we had to walk.
3. In "I think that I know him" the "*that*" is superfluous.
4. He died, *alas*, before the first performance of his great opera.
5. I promised to meet him *at* the corner of the street.
6. He offered the *ragged* boy sixpence to polish his shoes.
7. She *hurriedly* scribbled a note and sent Tom running off with it to the doctor.
8. Within ten minutes Tom *arrived* back with the doctor.

B. Use the following words to complete the passage below: *it, correct, alas, constantly, caused, generation, in, and*. The figures in the blanks indicate the parts of speech listed on page 40.

There is no such thing as an absolutely correct or standard English. The language is —4— in process of changing. What is considered —3— in one —1— may be regarded as totally incorrect in the next. This is true of grammar, slang and meaning, and up till fairly recently it was also true of spelling; but it is ironical that the most nearly standardized element —7— English is now its spelling. It might be a good thing to have a completely standardized spelling, if it wasn't that pronunciation tends to change, —6— ought to change with —5—. As it is, —8—, our spelling was standardized on an etymological basis in the eighteenth century and this has —2— many spellings to be quite unphonetic today.

NOUNS

C. The nouns, in the wrong order, are the names of the things illustrated below. Identify each one, and then state the class of things to which it belongs. The list of classes is given below the pictures.

Begin like this : 1. A frog is an amphibious animal.

clarinet	dodo	poplar	cypress	helicopter
crotchet	encyclopedia	lupin	kangaroo	frog
microscope	The Milky Way	swallow	elephant	corporal

a perennial plant

an aircraft

a marsupial

an extinct bird

a reference book

an evergreen tree

a deciduous tree

a galaxy

a four-footed pachyderm

a wood-wind instrument

a non-commissioned officer

an optical instrument

a migratory bird

a musical

an

museum	elephant	turkey	aviary
surgery	galaxy	chalet	mortuary
bunker	squirrel	kraal	posse
humpy	eyrie	fusillade	cicada
congregation	sett	bouquet	reservoir

D. Choose from the box the noun meaning a place
  1. where birds are kept
  2. where historical relics are shown
  3. where water is stored
  4. where doctors receive their patients
  5. where dead bodies are kept for a time
  6. where a ship's fuel is stored

E. Choose the noun that names the creature
  1. that trumpets and ambles
  2. that gobbles and struts
  3. that has transparent wings and chirps like a grasshopper
  4. that hibernates in its drey (nest) during cold weather

F. Now choose the noun that names a collection
  1. of people in a church
  2. of police constables
  3. of flowers to be presented to someone
  4. of stars in a band, indistinguishable by the naked eye
  5. of shots discharged by many firearms

G. Finally, give the noun naming the home
  1. of an eagle
  2. of a badger
  3. of an aborigine in Australia
  4. of a Zulu in Africa
  5. of a Swiss living in snowy regions

ADJECTIVES

This page will enable you to revise a number of adjectives used in earlier books.

H. Notice how the following sentence gives a very good idea of an *unscrupulous* person without actually defining the adjective :

> As a pawnbroker Mr Crafty was utterly unscrupulous, thinking nothing of lending £5 on an article he knew to be worth £100, and then appropriating the article when the customer failed to redeem it.

Now describe each of the following in a similar way, so that the meaning of the italicized adjective becomes vividly clear :

1. an *impulsive* child
2. an *arrogant* teen-ager
3. an *impartial* judge
4. a *fluent* speaker
5. an *arid* island

6. an *assiduous* pupil
7. a *contemptible* competitor
8. an *imperturbable* surgeon
9. a *luscious* pear
10. an *apprehensive* mother

I. Pair these as antonyms.
Begin : 1. prodigal–economical.

1. prodigal   direct
2. arrogant   unoffending
3. lenient   considerable
4. circuitous   meek
5. benevolent   backward
6. diffuse   permanent
7. precocious   economical
8. temporary   severe
9. delinquent   concentrated
10. negligible   malevolent

J. Pair these as synonyms.
Begin : 1. impregnable–unconquerable.

1. impregnable   discontented
2. cordial   disagreeing
3. circuitous   ludicrous
4. eccentric   needy
5. eminent   unconquerable
6. farcical   readable
7. disgruntled   roundabout
8. legible   friendly
9. indigent   odd
10. dissident   distinguished

flimsy	brittle	anonymous	disreputable
puny	cogent	beneficial	perishable
biased	temperate	insincere	inclement
jocular	tranquil	defamatory	adjacent
hazardous	stunted	substantial	apathetic

K. Select from the box the adjective that best describes
1. food that decays quickly
2. a rod of metal that breaks easily
3. a frock that is lightly and insecurely made
4. a climate that is harsh and unpleasant to live in
5. a plant whose growth has been checked or cramped
6. a child who is undersized and weak
7. voters who show no interest or enthusiasm
8. a letter when we do not know who wrote it
9. a garden that joins on to yours
10. a holiday that does you good

L. Choose the adjective that means the opposite of
1. candid   4. unconvincing   7. respectable
2. serious   5. complimentary   8. enthusiastic
3. extreme   6. dispassionate   9. negligible

M. Now choose the adjective that means much the same as
1. considerable   4. libellous   7. deceitful
2. forceful   5. humorous   8. perilous
3. prejudiced   6. equable   9. peaceful

N. Number the words in the box 1-25, and then divide each into syllables and show the accent. For example: *joc'-u-lar. de-fam'-a-tor-y.*

VERBS

O. Write all twenty verbs in one alphabetical list. (See page 140.)

libel	forfeit	concede	gesticulate
cavil	elicit	summarize	subdue
sally	accredit	circularize	ascribe
imply	abet	paralyse	reprieve
gauge	infer	dismantle	stagnate

P. Add to each verb in your alphabetical list its present participle and its past participle, e.g. *abet–abetting–abetted.* (For changes in spelling when adding a suffix, see Rules II, III, IV, V, VII.)

Q. Use a verb from the box to complete each of these sentences. Sometimes a different part of the verb may be required.

1. You need not write a full account of the meeting ; it will be sufficient to — it in half a dozen lines.
2. The drying up of the stream caused the pond to — and become covered with green slime.
3. Many scholars — Shakespeare's plays to Francis Bacon.
4. The condemned man escaped the scaffold by being — at the eleventh hour.
5. My constant questioning of the boy finally — a reply.
6. Even the most stubborn person has to — that the Earth is not flat.
7. The loud-voiced few continued to —, raising frivolous objections to these reasonable proposals.
8. Despite the heavy rain, we — forth and reached our destination by midday.
9. If the success of a play can be — by the applause on the first night, this new comedy should run for years.
10. The methods he used for — the native inhabitants might be described as tyrannical.

ADVERBS

R. Most adverbs are formed by adding –*ly* to an adjective. State the adjective from which each adverb in the box has been formed.

deliriously	principally	temporarily	execrably
facetiously	literally	voluntarily	impeccably
evasively	astronomically	arbitrarily	despicably
precipitately	hypocritically	dilatorily	incompatibly
amateurishly	influentially	literarily	irreproachably

S. Make adverbs by adding –*ly* to each of the following adjectives. (For spelling changes when adding the suffix, see Rules II, III, IV, V, VI, VII, VIII.)

1. diligent
2. selective
3. solitary
4. necessary
5. iniquitous
6. potential
7. gratuitous
8. quizzical
9. indisputable
10. infinitesimal
11. extraordinary
12. contemptible

T. Notice that adjectives ending in –*ly* present a problem. It is too ungainly to add another –*ly* to make the adverb: *He did it friendlily*. And it sounds awkward to use the adjective form: *He did it friendly*. It is therefore better to avoid the problem by rewriting: *He did it in a friendly way*. (*Early* and *daily* are the only –*ly* adjectives that can easily be used as adverbs, e.g. *He delivered the papers early*.)

Rewrite these to avoid the awkward adverb:

1. The children marched out of school *orderly*.
2. The boaster behaved *cowardly* when put to the test.
3. The landlady treated the young lodgers *motherly*.
4. When I met Thomas he greeted me very *friendly*.

Nouns, Adjectives, Verbs and Adverbs

U. For each of the following write its opposite from the box.

Nouns	*Adjectives*	*Verbs*	*Adverbs*
1. agreement	6. sound	11. gratify	16. boldly
2. admiration	7. natural	12. desist	17. hurriedly
3. appointment	8. courteous	13. disburden	18. concisely
4. removal	9. explainable	14. depreciate	19. permanently
5. unawareness	10. admirable	15. collect	20. candidly

Nouns	*Adjectives*	*Verbs*	*Adverbs*
consciousness	inexplicable	appreciate	leisurely
installation	dilapidated	disappoint	verbosely
controversy	contemptible	disperse	evasively
contempt	affected	persevere	irresolutely
dismissal	abusive	encumber	temporarily

V. Now choose a synonym from the box for each of these:

1. burden 　3. agreement 　5. decayed 　7. pretentious
2. scorn 　4. wordily 　6. rude 　8. enigmatical

W. Use the right word from the box to fill these blanks:

1. You are said to — when you go on trying.
2. When a person becomes — he begins to use vile language.
3. If there is a difference of opinion about some question and it is argued about, we say there is a — about it.
4. You adopt a policy — when it is meant to last a short while only.
5. A man behaves — when he lacks determination.
6. A crowd of people are said to — when they break up and go off in different directions.
7. We speak of the — of a television set when we refer to its being placed in position and wired up.

Prepositions

X. Notice the preposition used in each of the expressions and check with a good dictionary the meaning of any of the words you do not know. Then use each expression to complete one of these sentences. It will not usually be the infinitive that is required.

to dissent from	to be marred by	to be answerable to
to gloat over	to be averse to	to be intent upon
to connive at	to be devoid of	to be endowed with
to culminate in	to be sensitive to	to be impervious to

1. If you are — doing something, you are resolved to do it.
2. This rare stamp has one fatal flaw : it is — a tear.
3. If you — someone's wrongdoing, you wink at it and overlook it.
4. A person who does stupid things may be said to be — common sense.
5. He said that he was — no one, and so meant that he was not responsible to anyone for his actions.
6. If a person is — to criticism, he just does not feel it and so is not influenced by it.
7. He was — a great wealth of energy and could keep going long after the rest of us were tired out.
8. Because he was a modest man he was not — admitting his shortcomings.
9. His career — success when he was appointed managing director of the firm.
10. A miser is inclined to — his gold.
11. A person who is — public opinion takes notice of it and usually modifies his behaviour accordingly.
12. He said that he — the official view, and then proceeded to explain why he disagreed with it.

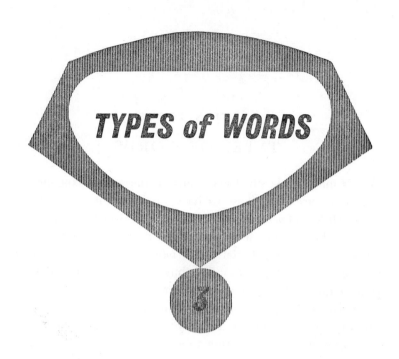

TYPES of WORDS

3

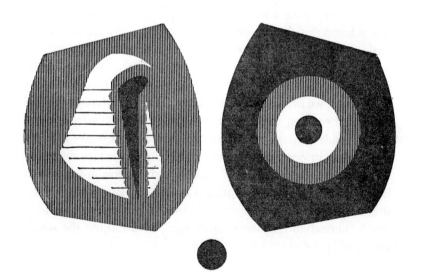

TYPES OF WORDS

Words may be classified according to the sort of language in which they are used. Thus we have nine different vocabularies :

1. *Ordinary Literal Words.* These are the words of our everyday vocabulary that have no hidden meaning but mean just what they say, letter by letter. When we call a spade a spade we are using the word literally ; but if we call it "a gardener's right hand" we are using words figuratively.

2. *Ordinary Figurative Words.* Whenever words are not used literally, they are used figuratively ; that is to say, they depart from their literal use in order to achieve a special effect. The two commonest forms of figurative language are the simile and the metaphor. If we say that a spade is like a gardener's right hand, we are using a simile. We do not mean that it is literally like a hand : it doesn't *look* a bit like one. We make a comparison in order to convey the special meaning that it is as valuable to the gardener as his own right hand. If we take the comparison farther and say that the spade is the gardener's right hand, we are using a metaphor. The words have departed even farther from their literal meaning ; we have transferred to the spade a name or description to which it is not literally applicable, in order to achieve a special effect. Usually when we speak of the gardener's right hand we are using words literally : we mean just that and no more. But when we say that a spade is the gardener's right hand, we mean something much more than the literal meaning : we are using the words figuratively.

We use many words figuratively in everyday speech. The word *leg* is used figuratively in "a leg of a chair", since literally a leg is a part of a living body. But the word has been used figuratively so long in this sense that we cease to think of it as figurative : it is a dead metaphor. And now we have used the word *dead* figuratively, since only things once living can literally be dead.

Some metaphors are so dead that they go back to a dead language—Latin. For example, the Latin word *explanare*, from which our *explain* comes, originally meant *to unroll* or *unfold*. When you unrolled your meaning you explained it. In this sense *explain* is a figurative word, but in fact we have forgotten its origin and now regard it as a literal word.

3. *Literary Words.* These are words that we do not use in conversation, but reserve for occasions when we are writing seriously or making a formal speech. Thus in conversation we might say, "The English army had a good go but was beaten". If we were writing a report in a history book we should be more likely to write something like this : "The English army made a valiant attempt but was vanquished". The latter sentence is literary and contains two words, *valiant* and *vanquished*, that are literary words, since we rarely use them in colloquial speech.

4. *Colloquial Words.* Colloquial language may be defined as the language of everyday speech. In this sense it includes both types 1 and 2 above. In fact, however, much of 1 and 2 is common to both colloquial and literary language, and it is better to define colloquial words as those of 1 and 2 that could not be included in 3. They are slightly "vulgar" and would be inappropriate on formal occasions. "We could do with more of it these days" is colloquial.

5. *Slang Words.* These are extremely colloquial, so "vulgar" as to be quite inadmissible on polite occasions. "Keep your hair on", "We had a smashing time", "That snooty

bloke thinks he's the cat's whiskers" are examples of slang. Some people would consider even "have a go" as slang, though others would say that it is now respectable enough to be considered merely colloquial. Indeed, many words begin as slang and in time become accepted as part of our polite language. "To cut no ice" was a slang expression when first used in 1896, and so was "to stage a come-back" when first used in 1920; but both are now respectable parts of our colloquial language.

6. *Poetical Words.* These are literary words used by tradition in poetry only, and may be considered a special form of type 3. Examples are: *thou, ere, oft, zephyr, the stilly air of eventide.*

7. *Technical Words.* Every occupation and activity has its own specialized terms with which the outsider is often unfamiliar. *Skiff* and *gaff* are technical words from sailing; *platen* and *galley-proof* from printing; *conveyance* and *testator* from the law; *pizzicato* and *chromatic* from music. Even *to be run out* is a technical term that would be quite meaningless, even nonsensical, to anyone not familiar with the game of cricket.

When a person uses the technical words of his profession too often, he is said to talk jargon. This may be all right in suitable company, but if an R.A.F. man, for example, uses Air Force jargon among those who "haven't a clue" it becomes bad manners.

It should be noted that some technical terms overlap slang. "Off the beam" and "go into a flat spin", for instance, are part of R.A.F. jargon, but they are also R.A.F. slang. It is worth remembering, too, that many technical words pass into and strengthen our general language. Thus "off the beam" has already passed into our general slang and may one day become fully acceptable colloquially. Similarly, "to score a goal" from football has already become a part of our everyday figurative language, while many technical terms, such as "visual aids" from education, "inferiority complex" from psychology, "acid test" from chemistry and "leading question" from the law have passed into both our ordinary literal language and our literary language.

8. *Commercial Words.* These are the terms used in business offices and correspondence, such as *herewith, receipt of, anent, the same, ditto, ultimo, even date.* Since business correspondence comes to almost everyone, it is arguable that these technical terms would be better discarded. They serve very little purpose, even inside an office, since ordinary English is just as serviceable, and outside they are an offence and should be resisted.

9. *Foreign Words.* These are simply foreign terms that have been borrowed, but have not yet been assimilated. If they are needed they will in time be thoroughly anglicized and become a part of our ordinary vocabulary. This is one of the main sources from which we enrich the language. Some words that still look foreign are : *status quo, négligé, bona fide, ennui.* We may recognize these as foreign too, but they are well on the way to becoming anglicized : *café, façade, matinée, fiancé, précis.*

Here is a short list of foreign words that seem to be in the process of becoming English :

ad infinitum, to infinity

chic, stylish ; in the fashion

ennui, mental weariness resulting from boredom

faux pas, a false step ; an indiscreet action

hors-d'œuvre, a dish before the main course

lapsus linguae, a slip of the tongue

négligé, free and easy attire

nom de plume, a pen-name ; a pseudonym

lebensraum, the space believed necessary for development

viva voce, an oral examination

EXERCISES

A. In the following passage ten words have been italicized. Identify the five that are used literally and the five that are used metaphorically.

The author said that if he were compelled to describe it shortly, he thought he would say that slang was experimental *language*. One authority had expressed a *doubt* whether any *exact* definition was possible. Another had *described* it as "a peculiar kind of *vagabond* language, always hanging on the *outskirts* of legitimate speech, but continually *straying* or forcing its way into *respectable* company". That description usefully likened slang to a linguistic *gate-crasher*. Like other gate-crashers slang was often thrown out but occasionally welcomed. When welcomed, it remained within the *pale*, and became part of our respectable company of words.

B. Use each of the following words in two sentences, first literally and then figuratively. Begin like this : 1 (a). There is an elaborate system of nerves connected with everyone's spine. 1 (b). The title of a book is usually shown on its spine.

1. spine   2. face   3. to sift   4. explosive   5. to fly

C. Pair each literary word with a more ordinary synonym :

1. intrepid	lodgings	9. cogitate	sin
2. deliberation	commonplace	10. appellation	Sunday
3. pertinent	fire	11. exorbitant	thin
4. banality	sweat	12. tempestuous	think
5. viscous	thought	13. animadversion	dear
6. perspiration	apt	14. transgression	name
7. accommodation	fearless	15. sabbath	blame
8. conflagration	sticky	16. emaciated	stormy

D. On the left are some very colloquial expressions, and on the right are expressions of similar meaning more suited to a dignified occasion. Pair them.

1. to take the rap   to come to an end
2. to get the boot   to his maximum capacity
3. to peter out   rather exorbitant
4. an awful bounder   a fanatically loyal supporter
5. for all he was worth   to be punished for another's crime
6. a bit steep   a likeable person
7. a smack in the eye   to be dismissed
8. a nice chap   a thorough scoundrel
9. a whole-hogging fan   not to offer any resistance
10. to take it lying down   gross discouragement

E. In the same way pair the slang expressions on the left and the polite expressions on the right.

1. to give 'em socks   to supply the information
2. to pep it up   to take the blame
3. to be browned off   to extinguish the light
4. to give the gen   to inflict great injury on them
5. to carry the can   to make oneself unpleasant
6. to be an awful bore   to make things more spirited
7. to shoot a line   to be swindled
8. to douse the glim   to be a great nuisance
9. to come the acid   to be discontentedly depressed
10. to be done brown   to be boastfully talkative

F. Choose a thoroughly English word from the second list to take the place of each foreign-sounding word in the first.

1. cognac 3. patois   5. annum   7. avoirdupois
2. ennui   4. resumé   6. excelsior 8. sobriquet
   weight   brandy   nickname   boredom
   dialect   year   higher   summary

G. Here is a list of technical terms, of which two are drawn from each of the following activities : music, law, architecture, physics, poetry, drama, war, sailing, religion, medicine. Place each word with its definition, stating the activity from which it is drawn. If correct, your list will be in alphabetical order. Begin like this : 1. Antiseptic (medicine) : preventing infection.

keynote	plaintiff	diagnosis	gamut
legacy	supersonic	lyrical	buttress
farcical	reconnaissance	theatrical	galvanic
berth	parochial	ballast	commander
façade	antiseptic	disciple	decasyllabic

1. preventing infection
2. heavy material placed in the hold to secure stability
3. a place where a ship can anchor
4. a structure built against a wall to strengthen it
5. a general or leader of a body of men
6. having ten syllables, e.g. "If Winter comes, can Spring be far behind?"
7. identification of disease by studying the symptoms
8. one of the early followers of Jesus
9. the face or front of a building
10. pertaining to dramatic work intended to incite laughter
11. causing or caused by electric currents
12. the notes of the musical scale
13. the chief note of a tune
14. that which is left by will ; a bequest
15. of or pertaining to poetry intended to be sung
16. belonging to a parish
17. a person who brings an action into court
18. military examination of a tract of country
19. travelling faster than sound
20. of or pertaining to dramatic performances

H. Writers of text-books sometimes put on airs and tell you
in forbidding tones that such-and-such literary expressions are
trite. They have been used so often that they lack freshness,
have become clichés and should be avoided. When you wish
to write at your best this is good advice : you should search for
the freshest, most telling words. But we cannot avoid some
trite expressions in our everyday notes and conversation, and
so we might as well at least know how to spell the words ! In
this exercise, you are asked to complete a dozen sentences by
the addition of the trite but serviceable expressions below.

too numerous to mention
from the sublime to the
  ridiculous
conspicuous by his absence
quiet reigns supreme
explore every avenue
in the last analysis

beggars description
a snare and a delusion
a chequered career
doomed to disappointment
the cup that cheers but not
  inebriates
proud possessor

1. This very lovely scene —.
2. The missing boy was —.
3. After — he at last gained success.
4. It is — to think you will never be let down by your
   friends.
5. The reasons for this are —.
6. When the children are in bed, —.
7. His unrealistic aspirations were —.
8. I am the — of a rather ancient car.
9. We must — till a solution of the problem is found.
10. —, building a vocabulary has its trials and tribulations.
11. The servant brought in the tea-tray and my hostess
    offered me —.
12. The orator went — by falling off the platform after
    making the greatest speech of his career.

I. Write the correct explanation after each of these foreign words or phrases :

1.	*à la carte*	arranged for this purpose
2.	*ad hoc*	to the point of disgust or satiety
3.	*ad libitum*	the characters of a play
4.	*ad nauseam*	God willing
5.	*au fait*	dressmaking of the latest fashion
6.	*bête noire*	to be left at the P.O. till called for
7.	*coup d'état*	a bugbear
8.	*Deo volente*	a head ; each
9.	*dramatis personae*	very well acquainted with
10.	*esprit de corps*	a person occupying another's place
11.	*ex officio*	a sudden decisive stroke in politics
12.	*fait accompli*	corporate feeling
13.	*haute couture*	the reason for a thing's existence
14.	*in camera*	at pleasure ; as much as you like
15.	*locum tenens*	by virtue of his office or position
16.	*mea culpa*	according to the bill of fare
17.	*per capita*	an intimate chat
18.	*poste restante*	my fault
19.	*raison d'être*	a thing already done
20.	*tête-à-tête*	in the judge's own room ; in secret

J. By referring to the appendix of an up-to-date dictionary explain the following technical terms :

1. an aqualung	6. balletomania	11. conventional weapons
2. an antibiotic	7. to bleep	12. a transistor valve
3. apartheid	8. centrifugal	13. crime passionnel
4. an autobahn	9. coexistence	14. a geiger counter
5. Benelux	10. cortisone	15. strontium 90

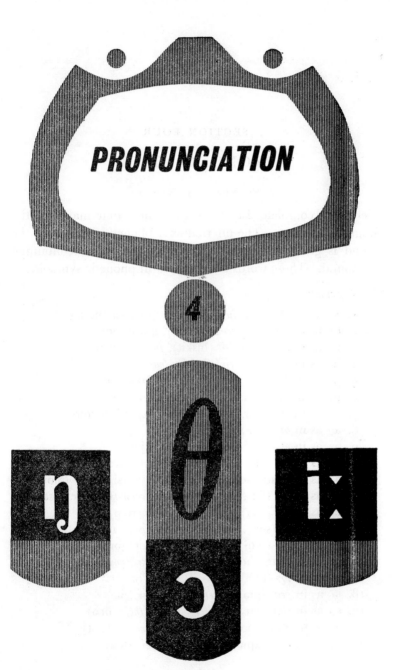

PRONUNCIATION

4

PRONUNCIATION

Sounds and Symbols

Here is a complete list of the 44 sounds that make up the English language. The international phonetic symbol for the sound is given and then examples of the words containing the sound. Those words are repeated in phonetic symbols.

Vowel Sounds

1. ʌ   as in *up* (ʌp), *clump* (klʌmp), *mongrel* (mʌngrəl)
2. ɑː   as in *art* (ɑːt), *graph* (grɑːf), *guard* (gɑːd)
3. i   as in *it* (it), *biscuit* (biskit), *forfeit* (fɔːfit)
4. iː   as in *tea* (tiː), *brief* (briːf), *league* (liːg)
5. u   as in *put* (put), *cook* (kuk), *woman* (wumən)
6. uː   as in *boot* (buːt), *glue* (gluː), *crew* (kruː)
7. e   as in *egg* (eg), *metal* (metəl), *leopard* (lepɑːd)
8. æ   as in *at* (æt), *snag* (snæg), *plait* (plæt)
9. ɔ   as in *on* (ɔn), *doll* (dɔl), *yacht* (jɔt)
10. ɔː   as in *all* (ɔːl), *cork* (kɔːk), *swarm* (swɔːm)
11. ə   as in unstressed *the* (ðə), *today* (tədɛi), *alone* (əloun)
12. əː   as in *fur* (fəː), *journey* (dʒəːni), *connoisseur* (kɔnəsəː)
13. ɛi   as in *pay* (pɛi), *eight* (ɛit), *reign* (rɛin)
14. ou   as in *so* (sou), *goal* (goul), *Moscow* (mɔskou)
15. ɑi   as in *my* (mɑi), *cider* (sɑidə), *awry* (ərɑi)
16. ɑu   as in *house* (hɑus), *howler* (hɑulə), *bough* (bɑu)
17. ɔi   as in *toy* (tɔi), *boil* (bɔil), *buoy* (bɔi)
18. iə   as in *gear* (giə), *sphere* (sfiə), *pier* (piə)
19. ɛə   as in *stair* (stɛə), *scarce* (skɛəs), *their* (ðɛə)
20. ɔə   as in *more* (mɔə), *coarse* (kɔəs), *court* (kɔət)
21. uə   as in *cure* (kjuə), *sure* (ʃuə), *doer* (duə)

Notes on Vowel Sounds : Vowels are the sounds produced when
the air passes through the mouth without obstruction. Consonants are the sounds in which the air is in some way impeded.
No. 11 is called the neutral vowel sound.   It never occurs in
stressed syllables, and in rapid speech it becomes the *ure* in
nature, our in *labour, ough* in *thorough, u* in *suppose, a* in *thousand, er*
in *pattern, ar* in *collar, or* in *actor, o* in *gallop, e* in *silent,* etc.
Notice also that Nos. 13-21 are made up of more than one
sound.   When two sounds glide together to make a single unit
we call them diphthongs.   Nos. 13-21 are diphthongs.

Consonant Sounds

22. p   as in *park* (paːk), *popped* (pɔpt), *happy* (hæpi)
23. b   as in *bark* (baːk), *burst* (bəːst), *bought* (bɔːt)
24. t   as in *tip* (tip), *bust* (bʌst), *Turk* (təːk)
25. d   as in *dip* (dip), *dare* (deə), *loved* (lʌvd)
26. k   as in *kill* (kil), *cap* (kæp), *chord* (kɔːd)
27. g   as in *got* (gɔt), *gun* (gʌn), *great* (greit)
28. m   as in *mat* (mæt), *mother* (mʌðə), *sum* (sʌm)
29. n   as in *nag* (næg), *nail* (neil), *nun* (nʌn)
30. ŋ   as in *sing* (siŋ), *long* (lɔŋ), *among* (əmʌŋ)
31. f   as in *file* (fail), *life* (laif), *rafter* (raːftə)
32. v   as in *vile* (vail), *live* (liv), *never* (nevə)
33. θ   as in *thin* (θin), *both* (bouθ), *method* (meθəd)
34. ð   as in *then* (ðen), *they* (ðei), *heather* (heðə)
35. r   as in *ran* (ræn), *rare* (reə), *around* (əraund)
36. s   as in *sat* (sæt), *place* (pleis), *cats* (kæts)
37. z   as in *was* (wɔz), *these* (ðiːz), *dogs* (dɔgz)
38. ʃ   as in *shut* (ʃʌt), *ash* (æʃ), *mission* (miʃən)
39. ʒ   as in *measure* (meʒə), *massage* (mæsaːʒ), *vision* (viʒən)
40. tʃ   as in *chance* (tʃaːns), *match* (mætʃ), *church* (tʃəːtʃ)
41. dʒ   as in *jug* (dʒʌg), *agile* (ædʒail), *manage* (mænədʒ)
42. l   as in *lack* (læk), *bale* (beil), *bulls* (bulz)
43. w   as in *way* (wei), *won* (wʌn), *women* (wimən)
44. j   as in *yes* (jes), *year* (jiə), *pure* (pjuə)

Notes on Consonant Sounds : Nos. 22-27 are made by air that escapes with a small explosion, and are called plosives. Nos. 28-30 are made by air passing through the nose, and are called nasals. Nos. 31-39 are made by friction of the air, and are called fricatives. Nos. 40 and 41 are made by a combination of explosion and friction, and are called affricates. In No. 42 the air passes round the sides of the tongue, and so *l* is called a lateral. Nos. 43 and 44 are called semi-vowels because the obstruction of the passage of air is so slight. Notice that No. 44 is sounded in a great many words where it is not represented by any letter, e.g. *curious* (kjuəriəs), *Muriel* (mjuəriəl), *pupil* (pjupəl), *cube* (kju:b), *few* (fju:), *ewe* (ju:).

Stress or Accent

In order to pronounce a word correctly, we must know not only the sounds that go to make it, but also where the accent or stress falls. The accent will fall on a particular syllable; so we must also be able to break the word into syllables. There is no problem with single-syllable words; but words of more than one syllable fall into the following main patterns:

(a) Words of two syllables with the stress on the first : *sis'-ter, pain'-ter, doc'-tor, a'-gile, for'-feit, her'-o.*

(b) Words of two syllables with the stress on the second : *be-hind', ob-scure', a-dult', be-gin', con-sist', mo-rose'.*

(c) Words of two syllables with both stressed : *thir'-teen', Chin'-ese', arm'-chair', back'-fire', half'-term', White'-hall'.*

(d) Words of three syllables with the stress on the first : *com'-i-cal, su'-i-cide, pos'-i-tive, per'-i-od, el'-e-gant.*

(e) Words of three syllables with the stress on the second : *co-loss'-al, de-lic'-ious, con-ges'-ted, ig-no'-ble.*

(f) Words of three syllables with the stress on the third, though sometimes there is a slight stress also on the first : *in-di-rect', dis-re-gard', re-par-tee', re-col-lect'.*

(g) Words of four or more syllables usually stress the third from last : *pho-tog'-raph-er, de-moc'-ra-cy, i-den'-tic-al, pa-ren'-the-sis, har-mon'-i-ous.*

Meaning changed by Shift of Stress

The position of the stress is so important that some words change their meaning or function completely with a shift of stress, as can be seen from this list :

1. *ab'stract* (adj.), considered apart from any application to a particular object ; not concrete
   abstract' (verb), to draw away ; to separate
2. *alter'nate* (adj.), done or happening by turns
   al'ternate (verb), to take or come in turn
3. *at'tribute* (noun), a quality or property
   attrib'ute (verb), to ascribe as belonging or appropriate to
4. *com'pact* (noun), an agreement between parties
   compact' (adj.), well-arranged ; closely pressed
5. *con'tent* (noun), what is contained in a book, vessel, etc.
   content' (adj.), satisfied with what one has
6. *con'vert* (noun) one who adopts a new opinion
   convert' (verb), to change into another form or state
7. *con'vict* (noun), a person held in prison
   convict' (verb), to prove guilty
8. *des'ert* (noun), a sandy waste
   desert' (verb), to forsake ; to run away
9. *es'cort* (noun), a guard for protection or honour
   escort' (verb), to go as a guard
10. *in'valid* (noun), a sick person
    inval'id (adj.), not valid ; without legal force
11. *min'ute* (noun), one-sixtieth of an hour
    minute' (adj.), very small
12. *ob'ject* (noun), a thing presented to the senses or the mind
    object' (verb), to oppose ; to give a reason against

13. *per'vert* (noun), a person turned from right to wrong
   pervert' (verb), to turn person or thing from right to
   wrong; to misapply
14. *ref'use* (noun), garbage
   refuse', to decline

Words often Mispronounced

acquiesce (ækwiés), to agree tacitly; to give way to
aerated (ɛəréitəd), charged with carbonic acid gas
aesthetic (i:zθétik), belonging to the appreciation of the beautiful
ague (ɛigju:), fever followed by fits of cold and shivering
asphalt (ǽsfelt), a kind of pitch used for paving, etc.
asthma (ǽsmɑ:), a disease characterized by difficult breathing
augury (ɔ́:gjuəri), divination from the actions of birds
Beethoven (bɛitouvən), a famous composer (1770–1827)
beneficent (benéfisənt), doing good
boatswain (bóusn), the ship's officer who has charge of boats,
   rigging, etc., and calls the men to their duties
boudoir (bú:dwɑ:), a lady's small private room
bourgeois (búəʒwɑ:), of or pertaining to the middle class
brochure (brɔ́ʃuə), a printed and stitched book containing only
   a few leaves; a pamphlet
brusque (brʌsk), blunt or off-hand in manner or speech
centrifugal (sentrífəgl), moving from the centre
Chopin (ʃoúpən), a famous composer (1810–1849)
circuitous (sə:kjú:itəs), indirect; roundabout
courier (kúriə), a messenger sent in haste
cuirass (kwiræs), a covering to defend the breast
cynosure (sínəzjuə), a centre of attraction
Derby (dɑ́:bi), the county town of Derbyshire
desuetude (dí:switju:d), disuse; cessation of practice or habit
desultory (désəltəri), without proper plan; jumping from one
   thing to another

dilettante (dilitǽnti), a superficial amateur with a smattering of
a subject

di'nghy (diŋgi), a small rowing-boat

dour (duə), stern; obstinate; hard

epitome (əpítəmi), a summary; a shortened form of anything

epoch (íːpɔk), a period of time; an era

extempore (ekstémpəri), improvised; done or said without
preparation

façade (fəsáːd), the face or front of a building

facsimile (fæksímili), an exact copy

faux pas (fou pɑː), a blunder, from the French meaning "false
step"

finale (finάːli), the end; the last part of a piece of music or of
a play

flaccid (flǽksid), limp; weak; easily pushed out of shape

forecastle (fóuksl), an upper deck before the foremast of a ship

genealogy (dʒiːniǽlədʒi), a list of a person's ancestors; the study
of pedigrees

Gloucester (glɔ́stə), the county town of Gloucestershire

gouge (gaudʒ), a curved chisel for cutting grooves

guerrilla (gərílə), irregular war waged by small bodies acting
independently

Haydn (heidn), a famous composer (1732–1809)

heifer (héfə), a young cow that has not had a calf

heinous (héinəs), giving great offence

incomparable (inkɔ́mpræbl), beyond compare

indict (indάit), to accuse; to charge with an offence or crime

inventory (ínvəntri), a list of articles

irreparable (irépərəbl), that cannot be repaired or replaced

itinerary (aitínəri), the route taken on a journey; a record of
travel

jeopardy (dʒépədi), a position of danger

joust (dʒaust), a fight with lances on horseback

Leicester (léstə), the county town of Leicestershire

limousine (límuːziːn), an old-fashioned type of motor-car

litigious (litídʒəs), fond of going to law

longevity (lɔŋdʒéviti), long life

mademoiselle (mædməzél), the French title for an unmarried woman

maelstrom (meilstrɔm), a great whirlpool

maniacal (mənáiəkl), insane, raving

migraine (míːgrein), a severe headache, usually on one side only

miscellany (miséləni), a mixture or collection of different things

misogynist (misɔ́dʒənist), a woman-hater

mocha (moúkə), a variety of coffee

mortgage (mɔ́ːgidʒ), to grant property as security

Mozart (moútsɑːt), a famous composer (1756–1791)

naive (nɑiːv), simple; without affectation

nausea (nɔ́ːsiə), seasickness; the feeling that one is about to be sick

Nemesis (némisis), punishment that surely follows sin

nonchalant (nɔ́nʃələnt), unconcerned; without a care

obloquy (ɔ́bləkwiː), abusive or contemptuous speech

obscenity (ɔbséniti), language or behaviour offending decency

obsequies (ɔ́bsíkwiz), funeral rites

obsequious (ɔbsíːkwiəs), cringing, fawning

omniscient (ɔmníʃənt), knowing all things

perfunctory (pəfʌ́ŋktəri), done carelessly

physiognomy (fiziɔ́nəmi), the face as expressing mind or character

piquancy (píːkənsi), the quality of being stimulating to the taste

plagiarism (pléidʒərizm), the stealing of another's writings

posthumous (pɔ́stjuməs), after death, e.g. a posthumous book

preferable (préfərəbl), to be preferred; more desirable

premature (prémətjuə), ripe too early; happening before the proper time

proprietary (proupráiətəri), belonging to an owner

psychiatrist (saikáiətrist), a specialist in the treatment of mental diseases

reconnaissance (rəkɔ́nisəns), military examination of a tract of country

reputable (répjutəbl), of good repute ; well thought of

requisite (rékwizit), necessary ; that cannot be done without

sacrilegious (sækrilídʒəs), violating or injuring sacred things

satiated (séiʃieitəd), fully filled ; supplied with too much

satiety (sətáiəti), the state of having enough or too much

schism (sizm), a division or split in a church, etc. ; discord

sinecure (sɑínəkjuə), an office giving a good income but little or no work

sleight (slɑit), quickness of action, e.g. sleight of hand

spinach (spínidʒ), a plant with leaves that are used for food

spontaneity (spontəní:iti), the state of being spontaneous

spontaneous (spontéinjəs), of one's own free will ; without apparent cause

statistician (stætistíʃən), a person skilled in statistics

statistics (stətístiks), facts and figures collected and arranged

superfluity (su:pəːflú:iti) the state of being superfluous

superfluous (su:pəːfluəs), more than enough ; not needed ; intended only for show

vehement (ví:əmənt), passionate ; carried away by one's feelings

Warwick (wɔ́rik), the county town of Warwickshire

EXERCISES

A. What words are represented by these phonetic symbols?

1. fɑː	6. kɔː	11. kɔːt	16. hɔːnt
2. kɑːd	7. tɔːn	12. kuːl	17. skwɛə
3. pɔt	8. sʌpə	13. súːpə	18. əkɔ́mpliʃ
4. pəliːs	9. kɔmə	14. ǽlibái	19. dʒuːil
5. sɔrou	10. θwɔːt	15. mǽsɑːʒ	20. ɔːdéiʃəs

B. Write the following words in phonetic symbols:

1. cots	4. plums	7. hero	10. plumber
2. dogs	5. plumes	8. heroine	11. pleasure
3. cloth	6. clothes	9. honey	12. stupid

C. Divide these words into two syllables each and show on which the stress falls. On four of them it falls on the first, and on the other four on the second syllable.

1. beside	3. acorn	5. useful	7. caress
2. prefer	4. welfare	6. frustrate	8. bulwark

D. Divide these words into three syllables each and show where the stress falls. It falls in equal numbers of times on the first, second and third syllables.

1. pianist	4. prohibit	7. irritate	10. decisive
2. diminish	5. understand	8. recover	11. interpose
3. afternoon	6. yesterday	9. entertain	12. innocent

E. Here are six words of four syllables, and six of five. Divide them into syllables and show where the stress falls.

1. congenial	5. etymology	9. subterranean	
2. impoverish	6. immaterial	10. simultaneous	
3. cordiality	7. perpendicular	11. inaugurate	
4. incompatible	8. illiterate	12. proprietor	

F. By consulting a dictionary, discover where the stress comes in each of the following words:

1. *August*, the eighth month of the year
2. *august*, lofty in tone
3. *contest*, to dispute; to compete for
4. *contest*, a friendly competition
5. *subject*, to bring under the power of
6. *subject*, any member of a state except the sovereign
7. *frequent*, to visit habitually
8. *frequent*, often

G. Certain combinations of letters look more difficult to spell and pronounce than others. The most difficult occur in words derived from the Greek. The reason for this is that the Greeks used an alphabet different from ours and it included several characters that can be represented only by a combination of English letters. This explains, for example: *ph* (Greek ϕ), hard *ch* (χ), *rh* (ρ), *th* (θ).

phase	chorus	rhinoceros	theatre
philosophy	choral	rhetoric	theory
pheasant	chord	rheumatism	theorem
pharmacy	character	rhododendron	theoretical
phenomenon	chiropodist	rhythmic	mythology

H. Find from the lists in G the words meaning:

1. anything visible; that which is perceived by observation or experiment
2. one of the changes in appearance of, for example, the moon
3. a person skilled in the care of hands and feet
4. the sacred legends of the different peoples of the world
5. the art of using words effectively in speaking or writing
6. the preparation and dispensing of medicines and drugs

I. Choose the right word from the lists on pages 66-69 to complete each of these sentences :

1. Some school playgrounds are laid with — to keep them hard and clean.
2. "The Magic Flute" was composed by Wolfgang — in 1791, the year of his death.
3. When Mr Jones was offered a knighthood he refused it on the grounds that it was — with his retiring disposition.
4. His apparently — manner helped to hide the fact that the forthcoming examinations alarmed him.
5. The report of the aircraft's safe arrival in Australia was —, for it has not yet reached there.
6. This — award of the Victoria Cross was deeply appreciated by the bereaved parents of the young hero who had lost his life.
7. The unexpectedly fine afternoon made umbrellas and raincoats —.
8. The monkey who climbed to the top of the flagstaff was the — of all eyes.
9. In spite of the heavy sea, they managed to lower the — and get away from the sinking ship.
10. Only by taking a — route did the hikers manage to avoid main roads and some of the larger towns.
11. The boy's — admission that he had not done his homework because he had not felt like it gave rise to some — remarks by the teacher.
12. The custom of wearing top-hats has so fallen into — that they are seldom to be seen.
13. At that time of the year, even one night's frost would place the whole of the strawberry crop in —.
14. The author of the book said that even criticism was — to being ignored.

J. You will observe from the lists on pages 62 and 63 that almost every sound in English may be represented by more than one letter, and every letter can represent more than one sound. The letter *s*, for example, represents the sound *s* in *sat*, *z* in *his*, and ʃ in *sugar*. Similarly, the sound *iː* is represented by *ee* in *seen*, *ea* in *speak*, *ie* in *believe*, *ei* in *receive*, *eo* in *people*, *i* in *machine*, and *e* in *scene*. The letter *a* represents:

(a) the sound in *cask, shaft, brass, graph*
(b) the sound in *village, furnace, private*
(c) the sound in *mass, latch, knack, fragile*
(d) the sound in *yacht, was, wanted, wan*
(e) the sound in *halt, waltz, pall, calling*
(f) the sound in *alone, apply, assisted*
(g) the sound in *wary, chary, varied*
(h) the sound in *cable, alien, bass, ague*

Now pronounce the following words carefully and place three of them in each of the eight groups listed above, numbering them (a), (b), etc.

apricot	hilarious	nefarious	able	attempt	vary
walnut	yachting	patriotic	ago	wallow	what
paltry	surface	luggage	chasm	ration	shall
tillage	ghastly	annoy	draft	apron	khaki

K. Now find

(1) two words in which the sound ai is represented by *i* and *y* respectively
(2) two words in which the sound k is represented by *c* and *ch* respectively
(3) two words in which the letter *g* represents the sounds g and dʒ respectively
(4) four words in which the letter *o* represents the sounds ɔ, uː, ou and u respectively

L. Many suggestions have been made for simplifying English spelling so that it will be as far as possible consistent with pronunciation. A passage from the speech made by Abraham Lincoln at Gettysburg in 1863 has been printed below in the new phonetic spelling recommended by the Simplified Spelling Society :

For-skor and sevn yeerz agoe our faadherz braut forth on dhis kontinent a nue naeshon, konseevd in liberti and dedikaeted to dhe propozishon dhat aul men are kreaeted eekwal. Nou we ar engaejd in a graet sivil wor, testing whedher dhat naeshon, or eni naeshon soe konseevd and soe dedikaeted, kan long enduer. We ar met on a graet batl-feeld ov dhat wor. We have kum to dedikaet a porshon of dhat feeld az a fienal resting-plaes for dhoez huu heer gaev dhaer lievz dhat dhat naeshon miet liv. It iz aultogedher fiting and proper dhat we shood duu dhiz.

1. Write out the passage in conventional spelling.
2. Study the new spelling carefully, and then try to write the following in it :

The new spelling has many advantages. It could be easily learnt by those used to the old, and it would help children and foreigners to learn English more quickly.

SILENT LETTERS

5

SILENT LETTERS

In English we have certain letters that appear in the spelling of words but are not sounded in the speaking of them. There are various historical (etymological) reasons for sounds and symbols being at variance in this way. In some cases the silent letter once had a sound. The *gh* in such words as *night, thought, plough* was in Anglo-Saxon times pronounced with a deep guttural sound; but with the coming of the Norman influence this sound was gradually softened till it eventually disappeared or softened into an *f* sound as in *cough* and *enough*. Yet we go on spelling the words as if the original guttural sound still existed. The silent *k* in *knife* and the *g* in *gnaw* were also pronounced in earlier times, as was the *w* in *sword*. All these letters are, so to speak, silent memorials of lost sounds. The process continues. In the long run we tend to pronounce words the easiest way, and today we find it easier to omit the sounds of *r* in *February* and *a* in *important*, so that these are in the process of becoming silent letters.

Sometimes a final consonant is silent because, like the *n* in *condemn*, it was in Latin followed by an inflexion (*condemno, condemnare*), but when it was taken over into English the inflexion was lost. The *n* cannot be pronounced without something after it, so it became silent. We give it back its sound, however, when we add a suffix, as in *condemnation*.

Sometimes, again, a consonant is silent because at one stage it was dropped in both pronunciation and spelling, and then put back again by the pedants. The *b* in *debt* is a case in

76

point. The original word was the Latin *debitum*, but it came into English through French (*dette*) and was so spelt by Chaucer. But scholars at the time of the Renaissance, knowing that the word derived from *debitum*, insisted on making it etymologically sound by giving it a *b* to show where it came from, and the *b* has remained silently with us ever since. The *b* in *doubt* (Latin *dubitum*) and the *p* in *receipt* (*receptum*) are explained in the same way. The extraordinary spelling of *victual* is similarly explained. It derives from the Latin *victualia*, but it came to us through the French *vitaille* and was spelt *vittle* till the scholars gave it a Latin shape.

The explanation of the silent *e* at the end of words like *love*, *live*, *have*, *give*, *above* goes back to the time when *u* and *v* had only one sign. To indicate that the consonant *v* and not the vowel *u* was intended, a silent *e* was attached to the consonant. This also explains why no true English word ends in *v* without an *e*.

Except after *v* the final *e* is not strictly silent. Although not itself pronounced, it has an effect on pronunciation. In words like *age*, *bridge*, *shape*, *edge* it makes the *g* soft ; without it the *g* would be hard. Similarly, in words like *slice*, *face*, *deference*, it keeps the *c* soft ; otherwise the *c* would be pronounced like a *k*, as in *picnic*. Then in the numerous words like *rate*, *bite*, *cute*, the final *e* makes the vowel long ; without it the words would be quite different—*rat, bit, cut*.

Here is a list of letters that are sometimes silent, together with examples of words in which they appear.

Silent *a* : aisle, extraordinary, parliament
Silent *b* : climb, comb, debtor, entombed, subtle
Silent *c* : descend, indictment, rescind, scent, sceptre, schedule, schism, scissors, scythe
Silent *d* : handsome, Wednesday (and usually now in *friendship, landscape, grandfather*)

Silent *e*: above, give, have

Silent *g*: campaign, champagne, condign, deign, diaphragm, ensign, gnarled, gnash, gnome, impugn, malign, poignant, sovereign

Silent *gh*: daughter, fraught, furlough, haughty, high, might, plight, plough, weight

Silent *h*: aghast, ghastly, gherkin, ghetto, ghoul, heir, honest, honourable, hourly, rhapsody, rhetoric, rheumatism, rhinoceros, rhubarb, rhythm, vehicle. (In southern English *h* is usually silent after *w*—*what, when, where*.)

Silent *k*: knell, knighthood, knoll, knot, knout, knuckle

Silent *l*: almond, almoner, alms, balmy, calm, folk, half, palm, qualm, salmon, would, yolk

Silent *n*: autumn, column, hymn, limn, solemn

Silent *p*: contempt, empty, exempt, pneumatic, pneumonia, prompt, psalm, pseudonym, symptom. (The *p* in *cupboard* is not strictly silent: by assimilation with the *b* of *board* it is pronounced *b*, so that it really has a double *b*—*cubboard*.)

Silent *s*: aisle, demesne, island, isle, viscount

Silent *t*: bristle, bustle, chestnut, christen, glisten, jostle, mistletoe, moisten, mortgage, ostler, thistle

Silent *u*: biscuit, circuit, conduit, guard, guillotine, guilty, guinea, guitar

Silent *w*: Greenwich, playwright, Warwick, wrangle, wrathful, wrestle, wriggle, writhe

It may also be noticed that in words of one syllable containing a double consonant one of them must be silent, e.g. add, Ann, ebb, egg, inn, odd.

EXERCISES

A. Find on pages 77 and 78 the words that have the following definitions. If correct, your list will be in alphabetical order.

1. struck with great fear or horror
2. the passage between rows of pews in a church
3. one who gives out charitable relief
4. a going round
5. adequate; well deserved (usually of punishment)
6. to condescend; to think worthy
7. any flat thing stretched across a hollow body
8. a small cucumber used for pickling
9. a demon supposed to feed on human bodies
10. twisted; full of knots
11. having a high opinion of oneself; looking down on others
12. to assail by word; to find fault with
13. a formal accusation
14. tending to cause evil; evil-minded
15. a plant that grows on the branches of trees, especially apple trees
16. a false name used by an author
17. a feeling of sickness; a misgiving; an uneasiness of conscience
18. to repeal; to annul; to revoke
19. a high-flown, enthusiastic utterance or composition
20. a list of names or goods; an inventory
21. the day of the week that derives its name from Woden, the Anglo-Saxon god
22. to take part in a noisy, angry argument
23. to twist the body about

79

B. Arrange the following words in groups of four according to whether they contain a silent *b*, *c*, *g*, *h*, *l*, *p* or *t* :

soften	foreigner	castle	yolk
gnawed	psalmist	almond	scientific
palmist	subtly	ghost	rheumatic
heiress	benumbed	succumb	ptarmigan
ascent	indict	should	sovereignty
pneumatic	indebted	sceptre	consignment
Christmas	pseudonym	rhyme	mortgagor

C. Try to complete this alphabetical series, using only words that contain a silent letter :

aplomb, ballet, climb, debt, ensign, forecastle . . .

D. Arrange the following words in alphabetical order, and supply a definition of each :

succumb	sobriquet	balm	corps	isthmus
crochet	apropos	phlegm	victuals	awry

E. A word crocodile is formed when the last three letters of each word are the same as the first three letters of the next word, as on the right.

poignant
antique
quest
estimable
blemish

Can you form crocodiles from the following clues? The first word in each contains a silent letter.

(a) 1. a social worker attached to a hospital
2. the state of having weak nerves
3. one who writes essays
4. a narrow neck of land joining two large areas

(b) 1. a formal accusation
2. a person who enters
3. two places on the opposite sides of the world
4. the act of going down

A short HISTORY of the ENGLISH LANGUAGE

6

A SHORT HISTORY OF THE ENGLISH LANGUAGE

The English language, as you well know by now, does not stand still. It is a living thing, and so is always in process of changing. New words are added whenever new needs arise; whilst old ones are discarded as soon as their usefulness has been exhausted. Still others change their form, their pronunciation, their meaning, to meet the ever-changing needs of the people whose invaluable servants they are.

Where have all our words come from? In a sense they have all been borrowed, and the borrowings have been most numerous whenever there was an invasion of one sort or another. A pure-bred English language has never existed; it is aggressively mongrel. To change the metaphor, it is an interweaving of all the borrowings and their derivatives down the ages.

We need go back no further than the time when Britain was inhabited by the Ancient Britons, who were really Kelts speaking Keltic. The number of Keltic words still surviving in our language is very limited, but probably includes: *bannock, clout, crock, dam, drudge, glen, hassock* (tuft of coarse grass), *knob, mattock, mug, pool, taper. Avon* and *Ex*, which appear in the names of rivers and both mean 'water', are two more words borrowed from the Kelts.

Before the Kelts were driven out of England they were invaded in A.D. 43 by the Romans, who stormed London, the capital, and ruled the country for several centuries. It is possible that during those years the Kelts picked up many

Latin words from the occupying troops. We shall never know how many, for the Kelts were illiterate and left no records, and both Latin and Keltic were swept away by the invasion of the Anglo-Saxons. Thus very few Latin words from this period remain in our language, and those few were mostly left behind in the names of places. *Castra* (a camp) appears in Lancaster, Winchester, Leicester; *strata* (a paved way) in Stratford, Stratton, Streatham; *colonia* (a settlement) in Colne, Lincoln; *fossa* (a trench) in Fossoway, Fossebridge; *portus* (a harbour) in Portsmouth, Bridport. Three common nouns borrowed from the occupying Romans are: *mile* (mille passus), *wine* (vinum), *wall* (vallum).

Then came the biggest invasion of all. By the fifth century A.D. the Roman Empire was in decay and the occupying forces in Britain could not prevent the Jutes from settling in Kent and the Isle of Wight in A.D. 449. A Saxon invasion in the west followed shortly after, and then came the Angles to the east. The Romans were in full retreat. The new invaders sent for their wives and families and quickly established their own language, traditions, religion and customs. They seem to have had little use for the Ancient Britons, who mostly fled to Wales, Cornwall and Scotland, where the Keltic language survived. Indeed, the newcomers called them *Wealhas* (foreigners), from which the modern word *Welsh* derives.

Because they were such dominating invaders, the Jutes, Angles and Saxons established their own language, taking over very little of Keltic or Latin. Thus if we are to speak of an original English language, this must be it. We call it Old English, but actually there were several dialects, and it is a curious fact that the dialect from which modern English is mainly descended was that spoken by the Saxons, though we call it English as if it were rather the language of the Angles. Even so, modern English is very different from any kind of

Old English, as you will see from this sentence written in Old English in A.D. 893:

'Hēr on ðysum gāere fōr se micla here, ðe we gefyrn ymbe spraēcon, eft of ðaem ēastrice westweard to Bunnan.' ('In this year the great army, that we have already spoken about, came again from the east kingdom, westward to Boulogne.')

Different though it is from Old English, our language today contains many words direct from it, and it is perhaps an understatement to say that modern English has merely borrowed from Old English when in fact there is a solid core of Old English in it. Indeed, most of our short, vital everyday words are of Old English derivation. Our pronouns, prepositions and conjunctions, and our forcefully direct nouns, verbs, adjectives and adverbs, are still mainly Old English in origin, as will be seen from this list : *and, bright, come, find, good, hand, in, it, quickly, Tuesday, through, trough, two, under, was, we, well, when, would.*

Old English was a highly inflected language with a complicated grammar. There were two classes of adjectives, each declined differently, and every noun had a gender ; the gender of the word for woman was masculine ! The number of changes in the endings of words (inflexions) according to their grammatical function was very large indeed. Modern English is very different, for our grammar is simple and has very few inflexions. Yet it has almost entirely descended from Old English grammar. What has happened is that there has been a gradual levelling out, so that inflexions have disappeared, leaving only one common ending. One inflexion to show the plural has, however, survived and is today *-s.* In Old English there were several (we have another surviving in *ox–oxen*), but the most common was *-as,* which appeared in both the nominative (subject) and accusative (object) plural of many nouns. In the course of time it became the ending in all cases of practically all nouns, and shortened to –s. The only other inflexion left today is the one to show possession (genitive). This survives from the Old English genitive's singular inflexion of –es, and is now shown by 's or s'.

Many other characteristics of English words may be traced to Old English and the way it gradually changed. The fact that we say, for instance, to ride but have ridden, to drive but have driven, is explained by a shift of accent leading to certain vowel changes in Old English even before it arrived in England; while another change in vowel sounds that took place in England between A.D. 400 and 700 explains why we say tooth but teeth, mouse but mice, long but length, food but to feed.

Old English, then, unlike Keltic, was never ousted. It remained at the centre of the growing English language. Nevertheless it was continuously modified by a succession of invasions, till, as we have already seen, it looks today as much a foreign language as French or German.

The first of those invasions was the arrival of Christianity from Rome with the mission of St Augustine in A.D. 597. As a result, Old English added a number of words of a religious character, for which no native words existed, such as altar (altare), bishop (episcopus), candle (candela), Christmas, disciple (discipulus), mass (missa), monk (monachus), priest (presbyter).

Towards the end of the eighth century the Danish Vikings started invading the east coast of England. At first they merely plundered and went away. Later they began to settle. Within a hundred years those settlements had grown numerous and had extended to other parts of the country, and had the invaders not been defeated in 878 by Alfred the Great, king of Wessex, they would have overrun all England. Yet the strength of these marauding Danes grew so great that from 1016 to 1035 a Danish king called Canute was actually king of England. But this invasion was long drawn out and, unlike the Anglo-Saxons, the Vikings did not drive out the natives; they settled among them and in the end adopted their way of life. The Vikings were absorbed into the life of the Anglo-Saxons, and so was their language. This was quite natural, since their language was not unlike that of the Anglo-Saxons. It was also natural that in the process of being absorbed into Old English, the Vikings' own language should have an effect on it. In fact the Danish or Norse languages gave English many new words and altered the pronunciation of many more.

We can see the influence of Danish especially in the names of places where the Vikings settled. The Danish word *by*, meaning a town, appears in Grimsby, Whitby, Selby; *toft*, meaning a holding, appears in Lowestoft; *thwaite*, meaning a clearing, appears in Crosthwaite, Linthwaite, Slaithwaite; *thorpe*, meaning a village, appears in the surname Thorpe (or Thorp), and in many place-names such as Scunthorpe, Goldthorpe, Mablethorpe.

Some of the commonest words that we owe to the Danish invasion are: *are, by-law, call, clip, clumsy, fellow, firth, get, hit, husband, knife, low, outlaw, take, them, they, want.*

The next invasion was similar but more far-reaching as far as language was concerned. William of Normandy conquered England in 1066 and rewarded his officers by making them lords of many of the English manors. For nearly three hundred years Norman French became the language of the English Court, nobility, law courts, learned professions and schools. Indeed, grammar-school pupils were taught in Norman French right up into the fourteenth century. But the common people and many of the remaining Anglo-Saxon nobles went on speaking their native tongue. There were therefore two languages spoken from 1066 till early in the fourteenth century. The native language was considered crude and was rarely used in writing, while Norman French was considered polite and fit for literature. But gradually, as the Normans became cut off from France and intermarried with the Anglo-Saxons, the two languages mingled and became what we call Middle English. Though much more Old English than French, the new language owed many hundreds of words to Norman French. It was held in sufficient esteem by 1386 for Chaucer to write his *Canterbury Tales* in it, and it is interesting to note that about 13 per cent of Chaucer's vocabulary was French in origin.

What sort of words did Middle English borrow from Norman French ? For the most part they had to do with the more polite and cultured life for which the rough-mannered Anglo-Saxons had few words. It is amusing to observe that while the peasant tended his oxen and called them by that Old English name, as soon as they entered polite society in the form of roast meat they became beef, from *bœuf*, the French word for ox. In the same way pig became pork (from *porc*), sheep became mutton (from *mouton*) and calf became veal (from *veau*). Other common words of French origin are : *abbess, abbot, assize, cardinal, charity, comedy, courtesy, draper, haberdasher, humour, justice, larceny, repentance, security, tragedy, trespass, verdict.* Many of these words look as if they come from Latin, and at one remove most of them do, because French is a language largely derived from Latin.

One of the results of borrowing so many French words is that we often have two words for the same thing, one being Anglo-Saxon in origin and the other French. Thus we have *to wed* (Old English) and *to marry* (Norman French) ; *kingly* (O.E.) and *royal* (N.F.) ; *meal* (O.E.) and *repast* (N.F.) ; *child* (O.E.) and *infant* (N.F.). Generous borrowings from various languages is the main cause of the wealth of synonyms in modern English. The most numerous synonyms came later from Latin, such as *amicable* (Latin) and *friendly* (O.E.) ; *paternal* (L.) and *fatherly* (O.E.) ; *regal* (L.) and *kingly* (O.E.) ;

virile (L.) and *manly* (O.E.) ; *vacation* (L.) and *holiday* (O.E.). It will be noted that the Old English word is usually more homely and direct and usually to be preferred, though the longer word of more recent introduction has its place on formal occasions. Thus *conflagration* might sound right in a history book, but we should call it "a great fire" in conversation ; and we should certainly cry "Fire ! Fire !" if one broke out, rather than "Conflagration ! Conflagration !"

Like the Danes, then, the Normans became absorbed into the life of the natives, and in the process their language was also absorbed, and its effect on Old English was to turn it into Middle English. It must not, however, be supposed that the new language was the same all over the country ; there were widely different dialects according to where it was spoken. It so happens that modern English has developed mainly from the Middle English dialect spoken in the London area. This was because it had the advantage of being spoken at Court and at the universities of Oxford and Cambridge. It was also the dialect used by Chaucer and popularized by Caxton's printed books. Yet the other dialects went on being spoken and written locally, and traces of them exist to this day, so that a man from Somerset, say, or Tyneside is readily recognizable.

Middle English was already a very hybrid language, having borrowed from Keltic, Latin, Danish and French. Because of this it was very different from Old English and much more like Modern English, as you will see from this example of Middle English taken from Chaucer's *The Monk's Tale* :

> But litel out of Pize stant a tour,
> In whiche tour in prisoun put was he,
> And with hym been his litel children three ;
> The eldeste scarsly fyf yeer was of age.
> Allas. Fortune ! it was greet crueltee
> Swiche briddes for to putte in swiche a cage !

The English language was destined to become still more hybrid, for the next invasion brought with it a flood of Latin and Greek words, many of which soon became permanently absorbed into our language. The full tide of the revival of learning called the Renaissance reached England about 1500, and was of course based on the recently rediscovered classics of Latin and Greek. The Latin language was held in such respect that for a time it became a sort of international language among educated people. When the Englishman, Thomas More, for example, wrote his *Utopia*, he wrote it in Latin, and for more than a century Latin was the only language recognized in English schools ! No wonder Latin words began to invade our language by the thousand. Most of them had a literary flavour when first borrowed, but in course of time they acquired a wider application. You can see what an important part the Renaissance played in producing the language in which we speak and think today when you try to imagine an English language without the following words, all of which were borrowed at this time : *accommodate, capable, capacious, compute, distinguish, estimate, experiment, insinuate, investigate, manufacture, manuscript, master, pagan, persecute, radius, senior, tradition.*

Ancient Greek began to be drawn upon too, but never to the same extent as Latin. Its importance can be gauged from the following selection of words that came in with the Renaissance : *apology, apostrophe, climax, drama, emphasis, encyclopedia, epidemic, episode, epithet, grammar, hypothesis, hysterical, paragraph, parallel, physical, synonym.*

This flood of words from Latin and Greek did not cease with the Renaissance but has gone on ever since. Whenever we have needed a new word to name a new thing or new idea we have tended to look to Latin or Greek, e.g. *aerodrome* (G.), *bicycle* (L. & G.), *cinema* (G.), *penicillin* (L.), *phenol* (G.), *radio* (L.), *radium* (L.), *telegraph* (G.), *telephone* (G.), *uranium* (G.).

One of our more recent new words, *television*, is a mixture of Greek (*tele*, from afar) and Latin (*visus*, vision).

We have already noticed how this borrowing gave us synonyms like *kingly* (O.E.) and *regal* (L.). We must now notice that it also gave us many pairs of words derived from the same Latin word, since the Latin word had often been borrowed earlier through a Norman French word (e.g. *royal*) that had itself come from the Latin. Thus we have *debit* directly from Latin (*debitum*) and *debt* indirectly from the same Latin word through French. Similarly we have *fact* and *feat* (N.F.) from the Latin *factum*; *mint* and *money* (N.F.) from *moneta*; *pauper* and *poor* (N.F.) from *pauper*; *secure* and *sure* (N.F.) from *securus*; *separate* and *sever* (N.F.) from *separare*. The meanings of these pairs have become curiously different and have helped to make the English language perhaps the most subtle and expressive in the world.

By the time the English language had digested its Renaissance borrowings by the middle of the seventeenth century, it had more or less taken on its present form as far as grammar, spelling and pronunciation are concerned. There have of course been slight changes since, especially in pronunciation; and we have noticed how this has meant that spelling no longer always agrees with pronunciation. But in general the language from 1650 on is essentially Modern English, and its main development has been that of enlarging its vocabulary and modifying the meaning of existing words. Thus if we regard the Renaissance as the last major linguistic invasion, we must not forget that there have been dozens of minor ones since, and they are still going on.

For example, the invasion of Italian culture, mainly in the eighteenth century, gave us many musical and painting terms, such as *andante*, *concerto*, *fresco*, *mezzotint*, *replica*. The (literal!) invasion of Dutch sea power brought us *bulwark*, *deck*, *dock*, *yacht.* The invasion of science, especially since 1850, has given us a host of new technical terms, such as *analysis, automatic, bacteria, electron, impedance, oxygen, refrigeration, supersonic, telescope.* Then there has been an invasion of American films, bringing in its wake words like *big shot, boom* (in the commercial sense), *bootlegger, commuter* (season-ticket holder), *crook, elevator, fan* (supporter), *frame-up, gangster, go-getter, graft* (political bribery, etc.), *gunman, guy, hobo, once-over, outfit* (group of persons), *pep, phoney, public enemy No. 1, racket, rough-house, rubberneck, set-up, spotlight, stenographer, sucker, yes-man.*

Here are but a few of the terms that gained currency in World War I : *big noise* (important person), *binge, blimp* (small airship), *breeze* (or *wind*) *up, bunce, camouflage, civvy, cushy, embus* (to put troops into buses for transport), *pill-box* (small fort), *quids in, scrounge, spot of bother, U-boat, umpteen, zero hour, zoom.* The end of World War II saw us with more additions to our vocabulary : *ack ack, airstrip, back-room boys, Bailey bridge, black market, black-out, blitz, block-buster, boffin, bulldozer, Chindits, dambuster, D-day, fifth column, Gestapo, G.I., Home Guard, jeep, lease-lend, near miss, paratroops, quisling, spiv, V.I.P., Waaf, wishful thinking.* There are many others.

Our Service men and merchants engaged in world-wide trade have brought back words gathered abroad. Foreign merchants have brought their native words with them and sometimes left them here. In this way there have been many invasions from the Indian languages, Malay, Turkish, Arabic, Persian, Russian, Chinese, Portuguese, Spanish, German, various African languages, and so on, all enriching what Ralph Waldo Emerson, the famous American philosopher, once described as "the great metropolitan English speech, the sea which receives tributaries from every region under heaven".

EXERCISES

A. The fact that *father, mother, brother, sister, son, daughter* are words of Old English origin suggests that our Anglo-Saxon ancestors were family people. If there were no other way of knowing that society was based on the family in those days, these derivatives alone would tell us. (Incidentally, the fact that *aunt, uncle, cousin* are of Norman-French origin suggests that it was not until William the Conqueror came to England that people here bothered much with the more distant relationships.) The following words also derive from Old English. What does each group tell us about the way of life of the Anglo-Saxon ?

1. cow, goose, hen, sheep, swine
2. arrow, axe, bow, shield, spear, sword
3. fish, oar, sail, sea, ship, whale
4. earl, king, knight, lady, lord, queen
5. smith, weaver, wright

B. The following words entered our language from Norman French. What does each group tell us about the influence of the Norman Conquest on England ?

1. bacon, beef, mutton, pork, veal
2. assize, embezzle, jury, larceny, perjury, plaintiff
3. aunt, cousin, nephew, niece, uncle
4. charity, confess, devotion, paradise, patience, salvation
5. banker, draper, haberdasher

C. Try to explain how we came to have the following pairs of synonyms :

1. friendly–amiable
2. drug–medicine
3. kingly–regal
4. ghost–spirit
5. waterfall–cascade
6. show–appearance

D. With the help of this section and a good dictionary, say which group of words below was borrowed from

1. Keltic through the Ancient Britons
2. Anglo-Saxon through the Jutes, Angles and Saxons
3. Danish through the Vikings
4. Latin through the Christian missionaries of the sixth and seventh centuries
5. Norman French from 1066 to 1300
6. Latin during the Renaissance, 1500–1600
7. Greek during the Renaissance
8. Greek in recent times
9. Persian
10. German during the nineteenth century
11. Russian
12. Indian languages during the nineteenth century
13. Italian of the eighteenth century
14. Arabic

(a) bazaar, caravan, divan, pyjamas, shawl
(b) fellow, husband, outlaw, their, them, they, wrong
(c) bungalow, calico, chutney, khaki, mulligatawny, polo, puttees
(d) banquet, baron, chair, county, servant
(e) Avon, clout, crock, glen, mattock, pool
(f) animal, circus, exit, junior, medium, senior, specimen
(g) climax, epidemic, episode, hypothetical, paraphrase
(h) algebra, almanac, assassin, hazard, lemon, orange
(i) ash (tree), field, foot, heart, mere, weald, Wednesday
(j) aluminium, dynamo, magneto, meteorology, seismograph
(k) concerto, falsetto, libretto, oratorio, pianoforte
(l) Bolshevik, commissar, pogrom, samovar, steppe, tundra
(m) carouse, hinterland, kindergarten, lager, plunder
(n) candle, cleric, creed, cross, idol, saint

E. From which language—Greek, Latin, French, Irish, Dutch, Spanish, Italian, German, Turkish, Malay—has each of the following groups been borrowed ?

1. alligator, canyon, mosquito, negro, renegade, sherry
2. buoy, cruise, sloop, smack, yacht, yawl
3. blitz, dachshund, to loaf, nickel, quartz, zinc
4. bosh (nonsense), coffee, horde, kiosk, tulip, turban
5. amok, bamboo, bantam, raffia, sago, teak
6. blarney, brogue, galore, shamrock, shillelagh, tory
7. apex, gratis, miser, radius, terminus, vacuum
8. blonde, etiquette, naive, nonchalance, programme, souvenir
9. balustrade, motto, serenade, sonnet, soprano, tenor
10. catarrh, epitaph, scope, theology, topography, utopian

F. Except for very formal occasions the expressions on the left are too pretentious.   Replace each by a simpler and less Latinized expression from the right.

1.	the vernal commencement	the nose
2.	an intimidating conflagration	a morning wash
3.	a cordial reception	truthfully
4.	with veracity	to drip sweat
5.	terrestrial felicity	the beginning of spring
6.	to exude perspiration	died poor
7.	a matutinal ablution	earthly happiness
8.	the olfactory organ	a hearty welcome
9.	to ingurgitate voraciously	an alarming fire
10.	expired in indigent circumstances	to swallow greedily

SECOND SPELLING-BEE

—Per—
perceptible
perforation
permanent
pernicious
perquisite
perspective
persuasive
perverseness

—Ghosts—
aisle
biscuit
czar
guarantor
pneumonia
rhinoceros
viscount
wrangler

—Cities—
Bordeaux
Bucharest
Copenhagen
Edinburgh
Marseilles
Melbourne
Philadelphia
Rio de Janeiro

—Science—
ammonia
apparatus
calorie
Fahrenheit
hydrochloric
permanganate
temperature
vacuum

—Language—
apostrophe
apposition
dialect
emphasis
etymology
masculine
monosyllabic
orthography

—Maths—
bisector
circumference
compasses
denominator
equilateral
quadrilateral
rectangular
theorem

—Dis– or Diss–—
disappoint
disdainful
disproportionate
dissembling
dissimilar
dissipated
dissuasion
distraught

—Persons—
Beethoven
Eisenhower
Haydn
Khrushchev
Mendelssohn
Roosevelt
Shakespeare
Tschaikovsky

—Oddities—
beige
buoyant
catarrh
choir
diocese
gauge
lieutenant
scissors

SECOND CHECK ON MEANINGS

If correct, your list will be in alphabetical order.

1. living both on land and in water (page 43)
2. concerning; about; in respect to (55)
3. blame; criticism; censure (56)
4. to consider as belonging to a person or thing (47)
5. a bunch of flowers (44)
6. undergoing many changes (59)
7. an expert; a man of taste (62)
8. out of repair (49)
9. disagreeing; at variance (45)
10. a squirrel's nest (44)
11. limp; weak; easily pushed out of shape (67)
12. causing or caused by electric currents (58)
13. giving great offence (67)
14. faultlessly (48)
15. harsh; unpleasant; rough; stormy (46)
16. wicked; unjust (48)
17. language of a special group of persons (54)
18. fond of going to law (68)
19. an animal that carries its young in a pouch (43)
20. a thick-skinned quadruped (43)
21. teasing; that makes sport of others (48)
22. to persist; to go on trying (49)
23. the effect produced by plucking the strings of a violin (54)
24. an evergreen shrub with large roselike flowers (71)
25. a nickname; an assumed name (57)
26. to become foul from lack of motion (47)
27. stormy; blowing with great violence; angry (56)
28. impregnable (45)
29. a nobleman next in rank to an earl (78)
30. on the alert; not easily deceived (73)

WORD-BUILDING

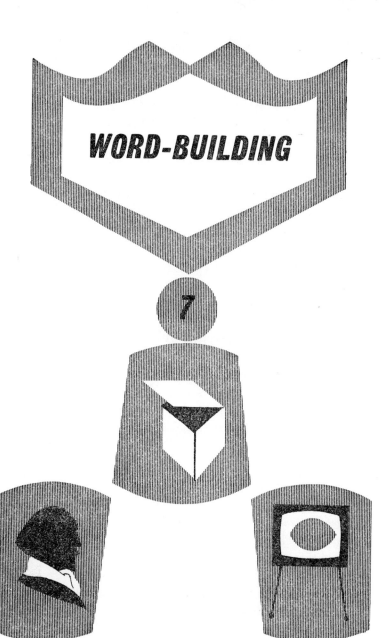

7

WORD-BUILDING

In the last section we were mainly concerned with the borrowing of words from other languages. But this is only one way in which a language builds up its vocabulary. It may also enrich itself from its own resources by a variety of means. Here are the main ones in English :

1. *By Compounds*. By joining two or more words together we are often able to create a single compound word that saves a much longer phrase. At first the compound is hyphenated, but when it becomes accepted it usually drops the hyphen. Numerous words have been and are still being formed in this way. Almost any combination of parts of speech is possible, as this list of examples shows :

noun + noun : gold-field, hailstorm, landmark, rainbow

adj. + noun : barefoot, blackbird, goldfish, two-thirds

noun + adj. : footsore, headstrong, house-proud, penny-wise

adj. + adj. : dark-blue, good-looking, half-dead, semi-nude

pron. + noun : he-goat, she-cat

gerund + noun : dining-room, fishing-rod, looking-glass

prep. + noun : aboveboard, outboard, outlaw, outside

verb + noun : cut-throat, kill-joy, makeshift, spendthrift, spitfire, spoilsport, treadmill

verb + adv. : farewell, send-off, standstill, walk-over

adv. + verb : income, outcome, outdo, outlive, overcome, undermine, understand

adv. + adv. : downtrodden, evergreen, ingoing, onlooker

adv. + prep. : hereafter, therein, whereupon

It is interesting to remember that most prefixes began life as prepositions. Some are still recognizable as prepositions and are almost indistinguishable from them. Thus in *afternoon* and *inborn* it is difficult to decide whether we are using the prefixes *after* and *in* or the prepositions *after* and *in*. This means that the methods of building new words by compounds and building them by adding prefixes are similar. It was the habit of using prepositions in making compounds that gave rise to the using of prefixes.

Finally it is worth noticing that English is such an adaptable language that we can make compounds of three or more words, as in *devil-may-care, happy-go-lucky, man-of-war, mother-in-law, nevertheless, notwithstanding, rough-and-ready, toad-in-the-hole.*

2. *By Verb Phrases.* In English there are hundreds of verb phrases, such as *cut out, give in, hang on, pull up, put up with, scrape through, turn down,* which have a meaning different from the sum of their parts, and new ones are being added every year. In these phrases the second word (sometimes there is a third as well) is not really a preposition or an adverb, but part of the verb itself. You can see this from these sentences :

(a) It is hard to *pull* a sledge *up* a hill.

(b) Should I *pull up* or down when operating this lever ?

(c) To *pull up* suddenly is bad driving.

In (a) *up* is a preposition, and in (b) it is an adverb. In both cases it has a meaning of its own. But in (c) it has no meaning of its own ; it is not a question of pulling up or down, or of pulling up a hill or down a hill. In combination with *pull* the word *up* here means to stop. Again, when we *wash up,* we are not doing the opposite of washing down ; we are engaged on the specific task of cleansing dishes and cutlery after a meal.

In the early stages of language these verb phrases sometimes became single words, e.g. *do off–doff, do on–don, do out–dout* (now obsolete). But in more recent times we have kept the two words separate.

Although verb phrases are very numerous, one phrase may have more than one meaning. Consider *let off* in these sentences :

(a) We *let off* fireworks on the 5th of November.

(b) Though found guilty, he was *let off* with a caution.

(c) He *let off* half the house to tenants.

Here are some further verb phrases with their meanings : *buzz off* (depart), *fit out* (equip), *get out of* (avoid), *look after* (take care of), *put out* (extinguish), *take after* (resemble), *turn up* (arrive).

3. *By Metaphor.* We saw on page 52 how a word takes on a metaphorical meaning. It does not give us a new word, but it does give us a new meaning. Thus the literal meaning of *face* in "Mr Smith's face" is very different from its metaphorical meaning in "the face of a clock" or in "the buildings that face the sea ". In the same way *pineapple* started life as a metaphor : it resembled the pine-apple or pine-cone in shape only. This is really word-making by change of meaning (see No. 11). Two examples of new metaphorical meanings taken from the technical language of sport are *bias* and *riposte*. A person with a bias is like a bowl (in the game of bowls) that is weighted on one side, while a riposte is a quickly returned answer, like the quickly returned thrust in fencing.

4. *By Slang.* In the course of time many slang words have become respectable and entered the language proper. The word *slang* was not used till about 1756; before that it was called *cant* and meant the secret language of the underworld of thieves and rogues. Here are some examples of the words that were cant in 1725 and have since become good English : *bet, cheat, filch, flog, fun, jilt, prig, shabby, trip* (voyage). When he compiled his Dictionary in 1755, Dr Johnson dismissed the

following as slang or "low words", as he called them : *coax, dodge, fuss, simpleton.* Today they are all quite unobjectionable. In 1912 *bogus, boom, rollicking, rowdy* were still considered slang.

Where do slang words come from ? In many instances we do not know, and it is possible that they are often completely new creations. Of others we know the derivation, and they are usually rather far-fetched metaphors aiming at a showy novelty of effect. Thus the slang word *stunning* in "She's a stunning beauty" is a metaphorical use of *to stun.*

Almost every English-speaking country has its own slang. As we have noticed, American slang is widely known through films. Australian slang is less well known but equally racy. "To come a purler", for example, means to have a bad fall, while "to bash the ear" means to talk incessantly.

5. *By Onomatopoeia.* This is the technical name given to the formation of words in imitation of the sound made. Thus the word *hiss* makes roughly the same sound as the action named, as do *bang, buzz, crack, crash, cuckoo, flap, mumble, pop, quack, splash, squelch, twitter, whiz.* These are mostly original creations. That is to say, they have no history, no etymology ; they are root words created to represent a sound. This is probably how some of the first human sounds came into existence, and we are still bringing more into existence today. Some recent ones are *ping-pong* and, both representing the sound of crashing aircraft, *kerdoink* and *prang.*

6. *By Shortening.* The shortening of words by the omission of sounds from the beginning, middle or end is a change in language that creates a new word, often but not always at the expense of an old one. Thus *sport* is a shortening of *disport*, but *disport* continues to exist as a word with a different meaning ; whilst *sample* is a shortening of *ensample*, which has dropped out of our language. Here are further examples of words that are shortenings of words that still exist :

bus (omnibus)	pram (perambulator)
cute (acute)	rhino (rhinoceros)
fence (defence)	size (assize)
loco (locomotive)	spite (despite)
miss (mistress)	venture (adventure)
navvy (navigator)	zoo (zoological gardens)

The sources of these shortenings are no longer used :

cheat (escheat)	scaffold (escafaut)	standard (estendard)
per cent (percentum)	sit (sittan)	ticket (etiquet)
proxy (procuracy)	stain (distain)	vie (envien)

Shortening is still adding new words to our vocabulary. *Bus* (omnibus, from the Latin meaning "for all"), *cycle* (bicycle) and *taxi* (taximeter cab, which is itself short for "cabriolet") are fairly recent ones to be accepted in literary language. *Bike* (bicycle), *demob* (demobilize), *exam* (examination), *fridge* (refrigerator), *maths* (mathematics), *phone* (telephone), *photo* (photograph), *rugger* (Rugby football) and *soccer* (Association football) seem to be well on the way to acceptance, though perhaps *gent* (gentleman), *mike* (microphone), *perm* (permanent wave), *prep* (preparation), *telly* (television) and *trike* (tricycle) have farther to go, and some of them may never arrive. It remains to be seen whether, when they do arrive, their source words begin to have different meanings from them.

7. *By Telescoping.* This is somewhat similar to shortening and we referred to it under Verb Phrases. Two words are telescoped to make a single word : *alone* (all one), *atone* (at one), *doff* (do off), *pinafore* (pin afore).

8. *By Wrong Attachment.* An *adder* was originally a *nadder*. The *n* of *nadder* was, however, so often wrongly attached that people thought it was *an adder*, and eventually the word was so written. Other examples are *apron* (a napron), *auger* (a nauger), *newt* (an ewt), *nickname* (an eke name = an also name), *orange* (a norange).

9. *By Portmanteau Words.* These are made up by joining part of one word to part of another in order to convey the ideas behind both words. Thus *electrocute* comes from *electric* and *execute*; *melodrama* from *melody* and *drama*; *radiogram* from *radio set* and *gramophone*. Lewis Carroll created a portmanteau word *galumph* from *gallop* and *triumph*. Indeed it was he who invented the word *portmanteau* to describe this type of word.

10. *By Back-Formation.* The word *editor* for long existed on its own without a verb. Because it ended in *–or* people thought it must have been formed from a verb *to edit.* There was no such verb : it was formed back from the noun *editor.* Another back-formation is *to nestle* from the noun *nestling.* Others are *to burgle* from *burglar, to conscript* from *conscription, to enthuse* from *enthusiasm, greed* from *greedy, to resurrect* from *resurrection, televise* from *television* and, jocularly, *to butch* from *butcher.*

11. *By Change of Meaning.* A *box* originally meant a *box tree.* Then it came to stand for a container made of boxwood. Today it means any wooden container. Its meaning has been changed by widening. Many words, however, have changed their meanings as a result of narrowing. Thus in the time of Chaucer a *fowl* meant any sort of bird. Gradually it came to mean a special kind of bird only—a *hen.*

We noticed in No. 3 another way of changing the meaning, by metaphorical use. There are many other ways. Sometimes a word comes down in the world. *Cunning,* for example, originally meant *knowing* in the sense of *skilful*; today it has come to mean *knowing* in a *crafty* sense. In ancient Greece an idiot (*idiōtēs*) was a private citizen, one who did not hold any official position and was therefore considered an ignorant person. Other words go up in the world. For example, until the sixteenth century *urbane* simply described a town dweller, but by the end of the seventeenth century it had come to imply the possession of polished, courteous manners, as it still does.

The word *nice* has undergone a series of changes in meaning. In the sixteenth century it had the meaning of the Latin derivation, "stupid". By the beginning of the seventeenth century it meant "wanton". Then it became "affectedly coy or reluctant". From that it took on the meaning of "over-refined". This led to its being used in the sense of "difficult to satisfy", and thence to "finely discriminating". We still use it in this sense when we refer to "a nice distinction", meaning a fine one. By 1800 its more usual modern meaning of "agreeable" had arrived.

One last cause of change must be mentioned. It is prudery or a false sense of refinement that has caused us to use *paying guest* for *boarder, passing* for *death, undertaker* for *funeral arranger, turf accountant* for *bookmaker, expectorate* for *spit, perspiration* for *sweat, stomach* for *belly, toilet* for *water-closet, manure* for *dung*. When we seek to hide the real nature of something unpleasant, we are said to commit a euphemism. Sometimes a euphemism can be justified. In certain circumstances it may be necessary in order to spare a person's feelings. But it can be overdone, and once it is started there is seemingly no end. Up to the end of the eighteenth century the Old English word *belly* was perfectly respectable. But "refined" people began to think it vulgar and used *stomach* instead. Now *stomach* too is becoming rather vulgar and the faint-hearted talk about *tummies* instead. After *tummies* what next? Perhaps in the end we shall come back where we started and use *belly* once more.

Changes of meaning, of one sort and another, have been extremely numerous, and they are going on continuously. This explains why some words have several quite different meanings, because in taking on a new meaning a word does not necessarily lose its old meaning. Thus the single adjective *hard* can now mean *difficult, diligent, energetic, firm, harsh, intoxicating, severe, unfeeling*.

12. *By Becoming Another Part of Speech.* A word that is normally one part of speech may take on a new use and meaning by being used as another part of speech. Thus *park* was first a noun meaning a grassland with a few trees. Then it meant an open space in which to put cars. From this latter meaning we have the verb *to park*, which is quite different from the original noun.

Sometimes an adjective comes to have the force of a noun by the omission of the noun. Thus *submarine* formerly was an adjective only. It was later so often used in the term "a submarine vessel" that the noun was dropped and the adjective became a noun. The following also began as adjectives only and later became nouns too: *offensive* (the act of attacking), *panic* (fear), *principal* (a chief or head), *wireless* (telegraphy).

13. *By Proper Nouns.* Not only nouns but also verbs and adjectives are derived from the names of countries, towns and persons, real or imaginary. A *guinea*, for example, was named after the Guinea coast, from the gold of which the coin (worth twenty-one shillings) was originally made. *Worsted* is the name given to a kind of woollen cloth woven originally in the Norfolk village of Worstead. To *galvanize* comes from the name of the Italian physiologist Luigi Galvani, who discovered galvanism (electricity produced by chemical action) in 1792. To *tantalize* is derived from Tantalus, who in Greek mythology was condemned to stand up to his chin in water that receded every time he stooped to drink. To torment him further, fruit was suspended just above him and it went beyond his grasp whenever he reached for it. Another word that comes from an imaginary character, this time from literature, is *quixotic*, meaning "foolishly chivalrous", like Don Quixote, the hero of Cervantes' story.

On the next page is a short list of other words derived from proper nouns:

artesian (type of well) from Artois in N.W. France

atlas from Atlas, who held up the universe on his shoulders

bantam (small fowl) from its origin in Bantam, Java

bayonet (blade attached to rifle) from Bayonne in France, where
    it was first made

bedlam (a scene of uproar) a corruption of Bethlehem, from St
    Mary of Bethlehem hospital, made into a lunatic asylum
    in 1547

bowdlerize (to remove "strong meat" from a book) from Thomas
    Bowdler, who published an expurgated Shakespeare in
    1818

boycott (to combine against) from Captain Boycott, an Irish
    land agent, against whom the tenants combined in 1880

bunk, bunkum (claptrap, humbug) from Buncombe in N.
    Carolina, whose member spoke needlessly in Congress to
    impress his constituents

canter (easy gallop) from the Canterbury Pilgrims, who pre-
    ferred this pace

cardigan (buttoned jersey) from the fashion set by the Earl of
    Cardigan in about 1855

cereal (edible grain) from Ceres, the goddess of corn

coach (a carriage) from Kocs in Hungary

currant (dried grape) from the vineyards of Corinth in Greece

dahlia (a flower) from Dahl, the Swedish botanist (died 1791)
    who introduced it from Mexico

derrick (hoisting machine) from a seventeenth-century hangman
    at Tyburn

dunce (slow learner) from Duns in Berwickshire, whence came
    John Duns Scotus (1265–1305), a reactionary schoolman
    who opposed the new learning and educational progress

epicure (one who has fine taste in food and drink) from the
    Athenian philosopher Epicurus

gin (spirit) from abbreviation of Geneva

guillotine (decapitating machine) from Dr Joseph Guillotin (1738–1814), who proposed its use during the French Revolution

guy (effigy) from Guy Fawkes (1570–1606), who conspired to blow up the Houses of Parliament

hygiene (science of health) from Hygeia, Greek goddess of health

italics (sloping letters) from Italy, whence it was introduced by Aldus Manutius of Venice in about 1500

January (the first month) from Janus, the Roman god who guarded doors and was represented with two faces, back and front

jovial (merry) from Jove's planet (Jupiter), which astrologers believed to produce good humour

laconic (terse, pithy) from Laconia in Ancient Greece, whose people (Spartans) were reputed to be concise of speech

loganberry (a soft fruit) from Logan, who obtained the fruit by crossing the raspberry and the blackberry

martinet (strict disciplinarian) from Martinet, a French army officer who devised a system of drill in the reign of Louis XIV

martial (to do with war) from Mars, the god of war

meander (to wander) from the name of a winding river in Asia Minor

mercurial (sprightly, volatile) from the planet Mercury, which was supposed to give a vivacious nature to those born under its influence

mesmerism (hypnotism) from Franz Mesmer (1733–1815), an Austrian physician who developed it

Morse (telegraphic code) from its American inventor, Samuel F. B. Morse (1791–1872)

nicotine (poison from tobacco) from Jean Nicot (1530–1600), a French diplomat, who introduced tobacco in France

panic (fear) from the Greek god Pan, reputed to cause it

pasteurize (to sterilize by heating) from Louis Pasteur (1822–1895), the French biologist

port (wine) from Oporto, Portugal, where it is shipped

rugby (football) from Rugby School where this kind of football was favoured

sandwich from the Earl of Sandwich (1718–1792), who ate meat between slices of bread to save his having to leave the card table for meals

silhouette (a portrait in profile or outline) from Étienne de Silhouette (1709–1767), French minister of finance, whose name became a synonym for anything cheap

stentorian (loud-voiced) from Stentor, the loudest-voiced warrior in the army besieging Troy

tangerine (small orange) from Tangiers in Morocco

trilby (soft felt hat) from *Trilby*, a novel by George Du Maurier

volcano (erupting mountain) from Vulcan, the Greek god of fire

worsted (woollen yarn) from Worstead in Norfolk where it was originally woven

14. *By Borrowing.* This is a major way of enlarging and enriching the language and it is going on all the time. But it is not, of course, from its own resources. We dealt with it fully and historically in Section Six.

15. *By Affixes.* This is the other major means of increasing our language and making it more supple and adaptable. We saw in Section One, page 15, the main ways in which affixes (prefixes and suffixes) are attached to root words to build new ones. A knowledge of this is so valuable that we have devoted a whole section to affixes and roots (see page 112).

EXERCISES

A. From what parts of speech have each of the following compounds been formed ?

    1. breakfast   3. hotbed   5. runaway   7. blue-eyed

    2. inlay   4. steamship 6. sitting-room 8. holiday

B. Match each of these double verbs with a single verb of similar meaning :

1. give up	enter	9. leave behind	admit
2. come in	support	10. get away	discern
3. set up	confess	11. let in	suspend
4. boil down	relinquish	12. serve out	abandon
5. own up	submerge	13. make out	reject
6. go under	encircle	14. turn down	doff
7. go round	reduce	15. take off	distribute
8. back up	establish	16. hang up	escape

C. Can you suggest two different meanings for each of these verb phrases ? Show the differences by using them in sentences.

    1. put out   2. let out   3. shut up   4. take off

D. Consult a good dictionary to discover from which words the following were shortened :

    1. chap   3. cab   5. piano   7. phiz

    2. splay   4. wig   6. chord   8. mob

E. The following expressions are now used mainly in their metaphorical sense. Explain where they come from as literal expressions. Then use each metaphorically in a sentence.

    1. to go off the rails   4. to peter out

    2. to blow off steam   5. to pan out

    3. to be crestfallen   6. to kick over the traces

F. By consulting a good dictionary, try to find out in what way each of the following words has changed its meaning over the years :

    1. vulgar   3. blackguard   5. awful   7. gossip (noun)
    2. silly   4. knave   6. let (allow) 8. awful

G. From which proper nouns have these words been derived? We have already mentioned four of them in this section; the rest you should find in the dictionary.

    1. academy   3. epicure   5. currant   7. gin
    2. bedlam   4. laconic   6. milliner   8. martial

H. Can you suggest more dignified phrases that would take the place of these slang expressions ?

    1. Buzz off !   5. right up your street
    2. keen as mustard   6. I smell a rat.
    3. It's O.K. by me.   7. Nab that bloke !
    4. a dead-and-alive hole   8. flat broke

I. In this section we have discussed fifteen different ways in which a language can build up its vocabulary. Find an example of each of the ways in the following list. Begin like this :
    1. "landslide" is an example of word-building by compounds.

idiot	pub	navicert
jersey	miaow	to scavenge
almighty	landslide	operative (worker)
ballyhoo	saturnine	to look down upon
distemper	an umpire	the long arm of coincidence

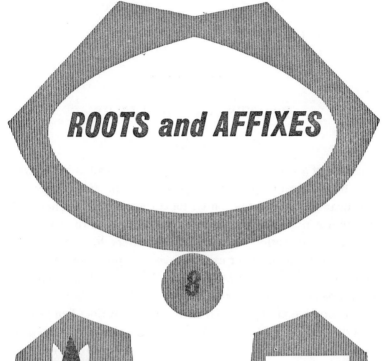

ROOTS and AFFIXES

ROOTS AND AFFIXES

Roots

The root of a word is the part of it common to all allied words ; it is the part from which they have all grown. Sometimes you also hear the word "stem" used for a root word. Technically, the stem is not quite the same as the root ; it is the root with any slight alteration or addition of letters to facilitate the adding of the suffix. For example, *emerge* and *immerse* have the same root (*mergo, mersum,* "I plunge"), but each is a separate stem : *emerge–emergence–emerges, immerse–immersing–immersion.* In this section we are concerned with roots as distinct from stems.

Old English roots showed the greatest power to grow new words before the Norman Conquest. Thus from the Old English verb *byrnan* (to burn) grew *brand, brandy, brimstone, brindle, brown* (burnt colour), *brunt.* After the Norman Conquest, when it became so easy to borrow new words from French, Latin or Greek, there was less urge to build new words from native roots. Hence, instead of making *starkin* (a little star), we borrowed *asterisk* from Greek. Here is a short list of words grown from native roots :

Old English Roots

beatan (to strike), bat, batter, battle, beat
beran (to carry), bairn, barrow, bear, berth, bier, birth, brood, brother, burden
bindan (to bind), band, bandage, bind, bond, bondage, bundle, woodbine

brecan (to break), bracken, brake, breach, break, breakfast,
  brick, brittle
ceapian (to buy), chapman, cheap, cheapen, chop
cwic (alive), quick, quicken, quicksand, quickset, quicksilver
dragan (to drag), drag, draggle, draught, draw, dray
faran (to go), far, fare, ferry, ford, thoroughfare, welfare
fleotan (to float), afloat, fleet, float, flotsam, ice-floe
foda (food), feed, fodder, food, forage, foray, foster
grafan (to dig), engrave, graft, grave, groove, grove
læran (to teach), learn, lore
sceran (to cut), score, scrap, scrape, scrip, share, sharp, shear,
  sheer, sheriff, shire, shirt, shore, short, shred, skirt
slagan (to strike), slaughter, slay, sledge-hammer, slog
stede (place), farmstead, homestead, instead, steady
tredan (to walk), trade, tradesman, treadle, treat
twa (two), between, twain, twelve (O.E. *twelf* = *twa* + *lif*, from
  læfan, to leave = two over), twin, two
wegan (to move), wag, wagon, wain, way, weigh
witan (to know), to wit, wisdom, wise, wit, witness
wyrt (herb), orchard (wortyard), wort

Speakers of English, however, decided that they could not
evolve enough new words from native roots to serve their
growing needs, and they resorted freely to the word-building
machinery imported ready-made from Latin and Greek. Some
people have argued that this was done too freely and that more
use of native roots could and should have been made. They
have suggested, for instance, that it would have been better
to make the word *folk-wain* instead of importing the Latin
omnibus, and to make *wort-lore* instead of borrowing the Greek
botany. Be that as it may, the advances in learning made a
purely Old English vocabulary impossible. Englishmen had
to borrow and build with Latin and Greek words to hold their
own in the new world. They may have overdone it at times,

but in the end the borrowings that stood the test of time became an integral part of the language. It was all done to such good effect that it has been estimated that about 13,000 English words today are derived from the 150 most common Latin and Greek roots. To the single Latin root *pono* (I place) no less than 250 English derivatives may be traced.

Here is a list of some of the most common Latin roots and the better-known English words derived from them:

Latin Roots

aequus (equal, impartial), adequate, equality, equator, equinox, equitable, equity, equivalent, iniquity

ago, actum (I act), action, actor, agent, agile, agitate

altus (high), altar, altitude, alto, exalt

amo, amatum (I love), amateur, amiable, amity, amorous

annus (year), anniversary, annual, annuity, biennial

aqua (water), aquarium, aquatic, aqueduct, aqueous

audio, auditum (I hear), audible, audience, auditorium

brevis (short), abbreviate, brief, brevity

capio, captum (I take), capacity, captivate, captive, capture

caput, capitis (head), cap, capital, captain, chapter

cedo, cessum (I yield), cede, concede, procession, succeed

civis (citizen), city, civic, civil, civilian, civilization

claudo, clausum (I shut), clause, close, conclude, seclude

colo, cultum (I till), agriculture, cultivate, culture

corpus, corporis (body), corporation, corps, corpse, corpulent

credo, creditum (I believe), credentials, credible, credit, creed

culpa (fault), culpable, culprit, exculpate

curro, cursum (I run), course, current, excursion, occur

dens, dentis (tooth), dental, dentist, indent, trident

dominus (lord), dominate, domineer, dominion, predominate

duco, ductum (I lead), conduct, ductile, educate, introduce

erro, erratum (I wander), errant, erratic, erroneous, error *facio, factum* (I do), fact, factory, feat, manufacture

finio, finitum (I finish), affinity, confine, definite, finite, infinite

flecto, flectum (I bend), deflect, flexible, inflexion, reflect

fortis (strong), comfort, force, fortify, fortitude, fortress

grex, gregis (flock), aggregate, congregate, gregarious, segregate

jacio, jactum (I throw), abject, inject, objection, reject, subject

jungo, junctum (I join), conjunction, joint, junction, juncture

jus, juris (law), jurisdiction, justice, justify

lego, lectum (I gather, read), collect, college, lecture, legend, legible

linquo, lictum (I leave), delinquent, derelict, relic, relinquish

ludo, lusum (I play), collusion, interlude, ludicrous, prelude

magnus (great), magnanimous, magnify, magnitude

manus (hand), manual, manufacture, manuscript

medius (middle), immediate, intermediate, mediate, medium

mergo, mersum (I plunge), emerge, emergency, immerse, submerge

mitto, missum (I send), commission, missile, mission, remit

moveo, motum (I move), commotion, emotion, motion, motive, motor, movement

nomen, nominis (name), ignominy, nominal, nominate

numerus (number), enumerate, innumerable, numerous

opus, operis (work), co-operate, opera, operation, operative

pars, partis (part), particle, partition, partner, party

patior, passus (I suffer), impassive, passion, passive, patient

pendeo, pensum (I hang), appendix, depend, pendulum, suspend

pes, pedis (foot), biped, expedition, pedal, pedestrian

poena (punishment), penal, penalty, penitent, repent

pono, positum (I place), apposite, component, deposit, imposition, opponent, position, post, posture, propose

primus (first), primary, prime, primitive, primrose

probo, probatum (I test), probable, probation, probe, prove

proprius (one's own), appropriate, proper, property, proprietor *puto, putatum* (I think, reckon), compute, dispute, reputation

rogo, rogatum (I ask), arrogant, derogatory, interrogate

rumpo, ruptum (I break), bankrupt, eruption, interruption, rupture

scribo, scriptum (I write), ascribe, inscribe, postscript, scribble

sedeo, sessum (I sit), preside, residence, sedentary, session

signum (mark), design, sign, signal, signature, signify

similis (like), assimilate, resemble, similarity, simile

struo, structum (I build), construct, obstruction, structure

tempus, temporis (time), contemporary, extempore, temporary

venio, ventum (I come), advent, contravene, convene, prevent

verbum (word), adverb, proverb, verb, verbal, verbatim, verbose

vivo, victum (I live), alive, convivial, victuals, vital, vivid

Greek Roots

dēr (air), aerial, aeronautical, aeroplane

anthrōpos (man), anthropology, misanthrope, philanthropy

arkhō (I rule), anarchy, monarchy, oligarchy

astēr (star), asterisk, astrology, astronomy, disaster

autos (self), autocrat, autograph, automatic

bios (life), amphibious, biography, biology

demos (people), democracy, democrat, epidemic

dunamis (power), dynamic, dynamite, dynamo

ēlektron (amber), electric, electrocute

gamos (marriage), bigamy, misogamy, monogamy

gē (earth), geography, geology, geometry

gramma (letter, thing written), anagram, grammar, programme, telegram

graphō (I write), autograph, calligraphy, geography, graphic

hudōr (water), hydrant, hydraulic, hydrogen

khronos (time), chronicle, chronometer, synchronize

kosmos (world, order, beauty), cosmetic, cosmos, microcosm *krinō* (I judge, decide), criterion, critic, hypocrisy

logos (word, speech, reason), analogy, catalogue, dialogue, epilogue, logic

metron (a measure), diameter, metre, perimeter, symmetry

monos (alone, single), monarchy, monopoly, monosyllable, monotone

nomos (law), astronomer, autonomy, economy, gastronomy

ōidē (a song), melody, ode, parody, rhapsody, tragedy

optikos (pertaining to sight), myopia, optic, synopsis

pathos (feeling, suffering), apathetic, pathetic, pathology, sympathy

philos (lover of), philanthropist, philology, philosopher

phōnē (sound), antiphony, euphony, phonetic, symphony

phōs, phōtos (light), phosphorus, photograph

polis (city), metropolis, policy, politics, Tripoli

polus (many), polyanthus, polygamy, polyglot, Polynesia

skopeō (I see), microscope, scope, stethoscope, telescope

sphaira (ball, globe), atmosphere, hemisphere, sphere, spherical

theos (a god), apotheosis, atheist, theology

temnō (I cut), anatomy, atom, epitome

Affixes

We have already noticed on page 15 how new words may be built by the addition of affixes (prefixes and suffixes) to root words. Prefixes, as we remarked on page 99, usually begin life as prepositions, though some of them are no longer recognizable as such since they have ceased to exist as anything but prefixes, while others may not be recognizable since they come from Greek or Latin. Derivatives formed by prefixes are usually the same part of speech as the root word. Thus we have *foreman* from the root word *man* plus the prefix *fore-*, and *mismanage* from *manage* plus *mis-*. The verb *becalm*, however, comes from the adjective *calm* plus *be-*.

Unlike the prefix, the suffix usually determines the part of speech of the new word formed. Thus the Old English suffix *–ness* was and still is added to adjectives to make abstract nouns (*hard–hardness*). You might say that *–ness* is a sign of an abstract noun. In the same way the Greek prefix *–ize* was and still is added to adjectives to make verbs (*human–humanize*), so that you might say that it is a sign of a verb.

Suffixes have been widely used ever since Anglo-Saxon days to build new words, and they have become an indispensable part of the language. It is interesting to note that at first only Old English suffixes were added to Old English root words. But as the new suffixes that came in with French, Latin and Greek borrowings became popular, people began adding them to the Old English. For example, *–ment* was a French suffix that came originally from Latin, but in the course of time it was added to the English roots *better* and *wonder* to make *betterment* and *wonderment*. Conversely Old English suffixes have been used to make new words from borrowed root words. Thus, *–ly* and *–ness* were added to *gracious* (Lat. *gratiosus*) to make *graciously* and *graciousness*.

The English language is very adaptable in this way. Prefixes too have been used with root words regardless of their origin. Thus the Latin prefix *re–* was and still is freely used with Old English verbs, and the language has gained by this convenience, as can be seen from this list of verbs: *rehouse, remake, rename, reopen, reshape, rewrite*. It has become natural to mix roots and affixes in this way, but when a new word is deliberately built from a root word and an affix, the scholar would shrink from mixing them. Nevertheless two deliberate hybrids have gained currency. *Bicycle* is a mixture of Latin and Greek, while *television* is a mixture of Greek and Latin.

Here are lists of some prefixes and suffixes that may be used, together with examples of words built with their help:

Old English Prefixes

a– (denoting *on*), abed, aboard, aloft, ashore

be– (to make), becalm, befoul, befriend, begrime, belittle

for– (negative), forbear, forbid, forgo, forswear

fore– (before), forebear, forbode, forecast, forehead, foretell

mis– (wrong), misalliance, misapply, mischance, misdeed, misdemeanour, misplace, mistrust

off– (from), offset, offshoot, offspring

out– (beyond), outbid, outlaw, outlive, outrun, outvie

over– (over, beyond), overdo, overreach, overseer, overthrow

un– (not), unaided, uncouth, undated, undone, unfair

un– (reverse), unclench, uncoil, undeceive, undo, unhinge

with– (back, against), withdraw, withhold, withstand

Latin Prefixes

ab– abs– a– (away, from), abduct, abjure; absent, abstain, abstraction; aspire, avert

ad– (to), adhere, advent; *and by assimilation*, accrue, affable, aggressor, alliance, annex, appeal, arrogant, assail

ante– (before), antecedent, antedate, ante-room

bene– (well), benediction, benefactor, benefit, benevolent

bis– bi– (twice), biscuit; biceps, bicycle, biennial, bifocal

circum– (around), circumference, circumlocution, circumscribe

com– con– co– (Lat. *cum* =with), commiserate, compound; conspire; coeval, co-operate; *and by assimilation*, collapse, corrugate, corroborate

contra– counter– (against), contradict, contravene, counteract

de– (down, away), deduce, depose, descend, dethrone

dis– di– (asunder, apart), dislocate, dispel, disperse, dissipate; digress; *and by assimilation*, diffuse

dis– (negative), disappear, disown, dissimilar; *and by assimilation*, diffident *ex– e–* (out of), exclusion, expulsion ; educate, eject, evade

em– en– (to make), embody, embolden ; enable, enlarge, ennoble

extra– (beyond), extra-mural, extraordinary, extravagant

in– im– (into), induce, invade ; imbibe ; *and by assimilation*, illumine, irradiate

in– im– ig– (negative), insipid ; imprudent ; ignoble, ignorant ; *and by assimilation*, illegal, irregular

inter– (between), interlude, intermediate, interrupt, interval

intro– (into, within), introduce, introspection, introvert

male– (evil), malediction, malevolent, malignant

non– (not), nonconformist, nondescript, nonentity, nonsense

ob– (against), object, obstruct ; *and by assimilation*, occur, offend, oppose

omni– (all), omnipotent, omniscient, omnivorous

per– (through), percolate, perforate, persist, pervade

post– (after), postgraduate, post-mortem, postpone, postscript

pre– (before), precede, predict, prefix, prelude

pro– (before, forth), proclaim, project, pronoun, protrude

pro– (in favour of), pro-British, pro-educational

quadri– quadru– (four), quadrilateral ; quadruped, quadruplet

re– (again, back), reaffirm, recreate, reflect, repeat, revert

semi– (half), semicircle, semicolon, semiquaver, semi-tropical

sub– (under), submit, subterranean ; *and by assimilation*, succeed, suffer, suggest, suppose

super– (above), superfluous, supernatural, supernumerary, supersede, supersonic, supervisor

trans– tra– (across), transatlantic, transfer ; traverse

tri– (three), triangle, tricycle, trilogy, trio, triplet

ultra– (beyond), ultramarine, ultra-modern, ultra-violet

uni– (Lat. *unus* = one), unicorn, uniform, unison, unitarian, universe

vice– (in place of), vice-admiral, vice-captain, viceroy, viscount

Greek Prefixes

a– an– (not, without), amorphous, apathy, atom ; anarchy

amphi– (around, on both sides, of both kinds), amphibious, amphitheatre

ana– (back, again), anachronism, anagram, analysis, anatomy

anti– (against), anti-British, antidote, antipathy, antithesis

arch– (chief), archangel, archbishop, arch-enemy, architect, arch-knave

auto– (self), autobiography, autograph, automatic

dia– (through), diagnose, diagonal, diameter, diaphanous

epi– (upon), epidemic, epigram, epitaph

hemi– (half), hemicycle, hemisphere, hemistich

homo– (same), homogeneous, homonym, homophone, homoplasm, homosexual

hyper– (over), hyperbole, hypercritical, hypersensitive

meta– (change), metamorphosis, metaphor

miso– mis– (hater of), misogamist, misogynist ; misanthrope

mono– (single), monochrome, monocle, monogamy, monologue, monoplane, monopoly, monotonous

pan– (all), panacea, pan-American, panorama, pantheist

para– (beside), parable, parabola, parallel, paraphrase, parasite

phil– (love of), philanthropist, philately, philosophy

poly– (many), polyanthus, polygamous, polygon, polysyllable

syn– sym– syl– (together), synchronize ; sympathy ; syllable

tele– (from afar), telegram, telepathy, television

Old English Suffixes

–ard –art (denoting habit), drunkard, dullard, sluggard ; braggart

–craft (skill), witchcraft, woodcraft

–dom (power, condition), freedom, kingdom, thraldom, wisdom

–en (diminutive), chicken, kitten, maiden

–en (made of), earthen, leaden, wooden, woollen

-en (to make), darken, enliven, fatten, quicken, soften

-er -ar -yer (doer, agent), farmer, printer; liar, scholar; lawyer

-er (comparative), cheaper, dearer, farther

-ern (direction), eastern, northern, southern, western

-est (superlative), cheapest, dearest, farthest

-fold (times), manifold, twofold

-ful (full of), artful, awful, cheerful, grateful, merciful

-head -hood (state, condition), Godhead; childhood, likelihood

-ing (verbal noun), farming, living, spelling, wedding

-ish (adjectival), bookish, foolish, girlish, sweetish, waspish

-kin (diminutive), catkin, jerkin, lambkin, napkin, pannikin

-less (without), penniless, reckless, ruthless, spineless

-like (like), godlike, lifelike, warlike, workmanlike

-ly (adjectival, originally *like*), kingly, manly, scholarly, soldierly

-ly (adverbial, originally *like*), brightly, cowardly, wrongly

-most (superlative), bottommost, foremost, topmost, uttermost

-ness (state, condition), blindness, goodness, happiness, holiness

-ock (diminutive), bittock, hillock

-ship -scape (denoting status, the quality of being so-and-so, from the O.E. *-scipe*), fellowship, friendship, lordship; landscape

-some (full of), irksome, tiresome, wholesome; *also* buxom (bow +some, bending like a bow)

-ster (agent), huckster, maltster, songster, spinster, tipster

-th -d -t (state, condition), dearth, health, ninth, sloth, width; deed, flood; draught, drift, height

-ward (towards), backward, forward, homeward, leeward, northward, windward

-wise (way), contrariwise, lengthwise, likewise, otherwise

-wright (agent), playwright, shipwright, wheelwright

-y (adjectival), dirty, earthy, messy, noisy, sulky

Latin Suffixes

–able (capable of), amiable, appreciable, deplorable, movable

–acious (full of), audacious, loquacious, mendacious

–age (abstract nouns), bondage, leakage, pillage, usage

–al (belonging to), general, legal, loyal, regal, royal

–an –ian –ain –en –on (denoting persons), pagan, publican; librarian; chieftain; warden; simpleton

–ance –ancy –ence –ency (abstract nouns), abundance, repentance; constancy; deference, diligence; consistency

–ane (adjectival), humane, mundane, urbane

–ant –ent (agent), assistant, claimant; agent, student

–ant –ent (adjectival), distant, militant; current, different

–ar (belonging to), circular, familiar, rectangular, singular

–ar –or –er –ier –eer (agent), vicar; author; preacher, usher; brigadier, collier; engineer, mountaineer, volunteer

–ary (belonging to), disciplinary, momentary, necessary, proprietary, sedentary

–ary (person or thing belonging to), glossary, granary, missionary, secretary, visionary

–ate (verbal), fluctuate, operate, renovate, venerate

–ate (adjectival), delicate, intricate, temperate, ultimate

–cy (abstract nouns), bankruptcy, delicacy, intimacy, obstinacy

–ee (denoting persons), absentee, employee, payee, refugee, trainee, trustee

–ery (place), bakery, fishery, nunnery, piggery, pottery

–esce (verbal), acquiesce, coalesce, effervesce

–esque (partaking of), burlesque, grotesque, picturesque

–ess (feminine), actress, conductress, duchess, tigress

–et –ette (diminutive), coronet, owlet, puppet; marionette

–fy (to make), magnify, rarefy, sanctify, signify

–ible (capable of), digestible, edible, feasible, flexible, tangible

–ic (belonging to), gigantic, metallic, public, rustic

–ice –ess (abstract noun), avarice, justice; distress, prowess

P. BK. VIII—I

–id (adjectival), acid, frigid, limpid, morbid, tepid

–ile (adjectival), docile, fragile, juvenile, mobile

–ine (belonging to), canine, divine, feline, saline

–ion –sion –tion (abstract nouns), dominion, opinion ; adhesion, vision ; consternation, emotion, relegation

–ior (more), exterior, interior, junior, senior, superior

–ive (adjectival), abusive, fugitive, furtive, plaintive

–lent (full of), corpulent, fraudulent, opulent, violent

–let (diminutive), booklet, ringlet, rivulet, streamlet

–ment (abstract nouns naming actions), arrangement, retirement

–mony (abstract nouns), matrimony, parsimony, testimony

–ory (place of action), dormitory, lavatory, refectory

–our –eous –ose (adjectival), nebulous, venomous, verminous ; miscellaneous, spontaneous ; grandiose, verbose

–tude (condition), attitude, beatitude, fortitude, lassitude

–ule (diminutive), globule, granule, molecule, reticule

–ure (abstract nouns naming actions), aperture, capture, closure, composure

Greek Suffixes

–ic (belonging to), aromatic, frantic, graphic

–ics (sciences), dynamics, mathematics, physics, politics

–ism (abstract nouns), atheism, baptism, criticism, socialism

–ist (one who believes a doctrine or practises an art or trade), atheist, botanist, chemist, florist, socialist

–ize (to make) (also *–ise*, see page 6), characterize, criticize, eulogize, philosophize. Now widely used with roots not derived from Greek, e.g. anglicize, nationalize

–y (abstract nouns), melancholy, monarchy, philosophy

EXERCISES

A. From which Latin roots on pages 114-16 do these come?
   1. ensign   4. civilize   7. captivate   10. manipulate
   2. verbosity   5. activity   8. deceased   11. co-operate
   3. annals   6. enamoured   9. postpone   12. dentifrice

B. From which Greek roots on pages 116 and 117 do these come?
   1. photograph   4. atomic   7. hypocrite   10. paragraph
   2. thermometer   5. asteroid   8. autonomy   11. aerated
   3. hydrophobia   6. optician   9. prologue   12. patriarch

C. Pair each of these nouns with the definitions below:

biologist	psychologist	accompanist	publicist
rationalist	opportunist	herbalist	satirist
economist	chiropodist	philatelist	oculist
fatalist	strategist	misogamist	geologist

1. one who accepts all that happens as inevitable
2. a hand and foot doctor
3. one skilled in the use of medicinal plants
4. one who writes on current social and political matters
5. one who studies the science of the earth's crust
6. a stamp-collector
7. one who takes advantage of prevailing circumstances
8. one who studies the science of physical life
9. one who studies the science of the human mind
10. one who founds his belief entirely on reason
11. a hater of marriage
12. one whose writings expose or ridicule vice or folly
13. one who plays an instrument while another sings
14. an eye doctor
15. one skilled in the art of war
16. one skilled in the science of production and distribution

atrocious	fallacious	precocious	specious
auspicious	judicious	pugnacious	suspicious
avaricious	mendacious	rapacious	tenacious
capricious	officious	sagacious	veracious
conscious	pernicious	spacious	voracious

D. Notice from the box that *i* before *ous* is necessary to keep the *c* soft. Now say what adjectives ending in *–ious* come from, or are linked with, these nouns :

    1. sagacity   3. vivacity   5. fallacy   7. malice
    2. capacity   4. audacity   6. space   8. delight

E. Make nouns ending in *–ity* from these adjectives :

    1. sagacious   3. atrocious   5. audacious   7. capacious
    2. tenacious   4. rapacious   6. ferocious   8. voracious

F. Select from the box the right words to complete these :

    1. An unsound argument can be described as —.
    2. A — man has an acute and discerning mind.
    3. We are — if we are fond of meddling with things that are not our concern.
    4. The word — derives from the Latin *pugnax*, which means "fond of fighting".
    5. A — argument seems convincing on the surface.
    6. A — person is one addicted to sudden changes of mind.
    7. An — beginning is one that gives promise of success.
    8. Those of — disposition are not easily turned from their purpose.
    9. The Latin root *ater*, meaning "coal-black", shows that an — act is one of dark brutality.
   10. One who speaks the truth is a — person.
   11. One who does not speak the truth is a — person.
   12. A — child is mentally in advance of his age.

G. Use one of the old English prefixes on page 119 to make a new word from each of these :

1. numb   3. trusting   5. flow   7. break
2. warned   4. sworn   6. lie   8. thwart

H. Find on pages 119 and 120 the English word derived from each Latin root and prefix listed below :

1. *medius +inter–*   4. *duco +ex–*   7. *facio +bene–*
2. *annus +bi–*   5. *venio +contra–* 8. *scribo +circum–*
3. *ductum +ab–*   6. *positum +de–*   9. *curro +ob–*

I. Do the same with each Greek root and prefix given below. The English words so derived are all on page 121.

1. *graphō +auto–*   3. *gamos +poly–*   5. *khronos +ana–*
2. *sphaira +hemi–*   4. *anthrōpos +phil–*   6. *pathos +anti–*

J. Make words by carrying out the following instructions :

1. In front of *–lent* write : excel, equiva, preva, indo.
2. In front of *–ment* write : retire, amend, bereave, incite.
3. In front of *–ful* write : remorse, disdain, resource, resent.
4. In front of *–ible* write : gull, leg, ed, suscept, fall, feas.
5. In front of *–ant* write : combat, contest, inform, descend.
6. In front of *–ist* write : extrem, reserv, lingu, ventriloqu.
7. In front of *–ary* write : solit, vision, custom, supplement.
8. In front of *–ate* write : specul, vacill, articul, agit, plac.

K. Notice that verbs derived from the Latin *cedo* are sometimes spelt *–ede* (recede) and sometimes *–eed* (proceed), but that the abstract noun is always *–ession* (recession, procession). Now form an abstract noun ending in *–sion* from each of these verbs :

1. proceed   3. concede   5. succeed   7. accede
2. cede   4. intercede   6. recede   8. secede

L. Complete this table :

Noun	Verb	Adjective	Adverb
1. courage	encourage	courageous	courageously
2. credit	accredit	—	creditably
3. crime	incriminate	criminal	—
4. custom	accustom	—	customarily
5. —	energize	—	energetically
6. force	enforce	forcible	—
7. —	fructify	—	fruitfully
8. —	glorify	glorious	—
9. —	harmonize	—	harmoniously
10. —	luxuriate	luxurious	—
11. name	nominate	—	nominally
12. —	enumerate	numerous	—
13. peril	—	perilous	—
14. poverty	impoverish	—	—
15. preparation	—	—	preparatorily
16. punishment	—	punitive	—
17. receipt	—	—	receptively
18. rarity	rarefy	—	—
19. reality	realize	—	—
20. repentance	—	—	repentantly
21. resonance	—	—	resonantly
22. retention	—	retentive	—
23. secrecy	secrete	—	—
24. stealth	—	—	stealthily
25. studiousness	—	—	—
26. stupidity	stupefy	—	—
27. —	substantiate	—	substantially
28. —	—	—	successfully
29. —	systematize	—	—
30. —	vitalize	—	—
31. width	—	—	—

M. Here are five ways of building new words:
  (a) Prefix +root (re +turn = return)
  (b) Root +suffix (hope +ful = hopeful)
  (c) Root +suffix +suffix (hope +ful +ly = hopefully)
  (d) Prefix +root +suffix (un +hope +ful = unhopeful)
  (e) Prefix +root +suffix +suffix (un +hope +ful +ly
       = unhopefully)

Now find four examples of each way in the following list, and
show how each word is built:

careless	transport	manly	warlike
monotone	transportable	girlhood	telegraph
boastfully	restlessness	embodiment	unhelpfulness
helplessly	displacement	mis-spelling	independently
argumentative	hemisphere	unbelievably	denationalize

N. Notice that the abstract noun formed from *include* is *in-
clusion*. Now form abstract nouns from:

  1. conclude   3. exclude   5. intrude   7. collude
  2. allude   4. delude   6. obtrude   8. seclude

O. The following words were all derived by adding a suffix to
a verb ending in mute *e*. Give the verb in each instance.

  1. enclosure   4. infringement   7. communication
  2. disciplining 5. disparagement   8. procrastination
  3. fascination   6. collapsible   9. accumulative

P. Make adverbs from the following adjectives:

  1. efficient   3. distrustful   5. infallible   7. intricate
  2. malevolent   4. indolent   6. illegible   8. momentary

Q. Abstract nouns formed from adjectives ending in *–ient*
sometimes end in *–ence* and sometimes in *–ency*. Form abstract
nouns from the following and check with a dictionary:

  1. disobedient   3 resilient   5. lenient   7. proficient
  2. inefficient   4. patient   6. expedient   8. transient

substantial	imperial	menial	perennial
credentials	pictorial	colonial	biennial
residential	colloquial	secretarial	matrimonial
influential	celestial	aerial	testimonial
inconsequential	editorial	memorial	marsupial

R. Notice that *ti* in the words in the first column is always pronounced like *sh*. This is natural, since *substantial*, for example, comes from a noun ending in *–ce* (substance). Give the nouns in *–ce* from which each of the following is formed:

    1. residential 2. influential 3. essential 4. confidential

S. Use a word from the box to fill each of these blanks:
    1. If you live at the place of work you have a — post.
    2. Everyday speech is —, not formal language.
    3. The kangaroo is a — because it carries its young in a pouch.
    4. — are letters of introduction.
    5. A servant is sometimes employed to carry out the — tasks in a household.
    6. The iris is known as a hardy — because it lives for more than two years.
    7. Being unmarried, a bachelor has no — responsibilities.
    8. An — remark is one that does not sensibly follow on.

T. *Testimonial* has been formed by adding *–al* to *testimony*. From what word ending in *y* does each of these come?

    1. memorial 3. secretarial 5. matrimonial 7. denial
    2. burial   4. colonial   6. industrial   8. ceremonial

WORD STORIES

9

WORD STORIES

Just to explain the derivation and formation of a word (its etymology) is in a sense to tell its story; and in this sense we have already related the stories of many words. But some words have specially interesting stories, and in this section we have picked out a few to show the fascination that word-study has for those scholars with the qualifications to pursue it.

The word *etymology* itself is not particularly interesting. By the time English scholars began to study words seriously and so need a word for that study, the French had already one in use. They spelt it *ethimologie* (modern, *étymologie*) and had borrowed it from the Greek *etumologia*, which was made up of *etumon* (true) and *logos* (word). English scholars took over the French word and in due course anglicized it by dropping the *h*, since *th* is pronounced *t* in French, and ending it with *y*.

A more interesting word is *diary*. Although it comes straight from the Latin word *diarium*, there is a story behind the Latin word. A *diarium* originally meant a daily allowance of food or pay given to Roman soldiers or workmen. Before long the word was applied to the note-book in which such daily items were recorded. Later still it came to mean a note-book for recording any daily occurrences or observations, and that is the meaning it kept when taken into the English language. The Latin word itself was formed from the word *dies* meaning a day. From this root word several of our own words have been derived. Thus *dial* is a plate showing the day marked out in hours, and *diurnal* means belonging to the day as opposed to the night. The word derived from Latin and meaning belonging to the night is *nocturnal*.

The story of the word *pecuniary* goes back even farther and throws light on one of the very early periods in the development of civilized man. In ancient times the Romans paid their debts with cattle. The ox was the unit of money in those days, just as the pound is today in Britain. Later, with the progress of civilization, money in its modern shape was invented, and it took the form of blocks of copper, each cast with the figure of an ox on it to indicate its value. Thus *pecus*, the Latin for "cattle", gave the Romans their word *pecunia* (money). It is no coincidence that our word *fee* comes from the Old English *feoh*, meaning cattle, in much the same way. From the word *pecunia* comes our adjective *pecuniary*, meaning "to do with money", "financial". It is used facetiously in the expression "pecuniary difficulties", but is otherwise a solemn word. Another adjective formed from *pecunia* is *impecunious*, and this too is usually reserved for humorous references to "impecunious circumstances". More useful words are *finance* and *financial*, derived from the Norman French *finer*, "to end or settle". But the truly homely word is *money*, which can be used as an adjective as well as a noun, as in "money matters". It was borrowed from the Romans in Anglo-Saxon times, and came from the Latin *moneta*, originally the name of the goddess in whose Roman temple money was coined. It thus meant a mint, and our own word *mint* derives from the same Latin word, but by a different route.

Although we sometimes use the word *money* as an adjective, it is not a full adjective and at times we are obliged to use *pecuniary* instead. Yet there is no noun meaning money to go alongside *pecuniary*. This oddness is even more noticeable with *sun* and *solar*. We use the Old English *sun* as the noun, but the only real adjective meaning "to do with the sun" is *solar*, derived from the Latin *solaris*. This explains why in English there are a number of adjectives that are nothing like the nouns they correspond to. Other examples are: *cat–feline, cow–bovine, dog–canine, eagle–aquiline, ear–aural, eye–ocular, house–domestic, moon–lunar, spring–vernal, star–stellar.*

Sometimes, however, there is one adjective from Old English and another from Latin. Thus we have *earthly* from Old English and *terrestrial* from Latin, both meaning much the same. More examples are: *blood–bloody–sanguinary, body–bodily–corporal–corporeal, brother–brotherly–fraternal, father–fatherly–paternal, hell–hellish–infernal, law–lawful–legal, praise–praiseworthy–laudable, word–wordy–verbose.*

Even in these last examples the pairs of adjectives are not 100 per cent synonymous. There are times when you could use *infernal* but not *hellish*. For instance, it might be right to refer to "the infernal regions" in Roman mythology, but wrong to call them "the hellish regions". Again, consider the difference between "lawful proceedings" and "legal proceedings".

Other adjectives have parted company almost completely, e.g. *air–airy–aerial, boy–boyish–puerile, cat–catty* (or *cattish*)–*feline, hand–handy–manual, home–homely–domestic, horse–horsey–equine, night–nightly–nocturnal, nose–nosey–nasal, sight–sightly–visual, sun–sunny–solar, water–watery–aquatic.*

A word with a wholly Old English story is *thrill*. In Anglo-Saxon days it was spelt ðȳrel (pronounced *theerel*) and meant a hole. We still have this meaning of the word in the second part of *nostril*, a word that literally meant "nose-hole". Later the Old English word was used as a verb meaning "to pierce or make holes in". Even as late as the early seventeenth century Shakespeare could still speak of "thrilling" a person with a sword. At some stage it was used metaphorically to mean that someone was pierced through or thrilled with excitement. It has now lost its literal meaning altogether but is all too frequently used in its metaphorical sense, both as a noun (a thrill) and as a verb (to thrill).

Other Old English words with interesting stories are: *bonfire*, which was originally *bone-fire*; *daisy*, which started as *day's eye* (*dæges ēage*); *lord*, which originally meant *loaf-guardian* (*hlāfweard*); *lady*, which once meant *loaf-kneader* (*hlāfdige*); *woman*, which was spelt *wifman* in Anglo-Saxon days.

Glamour is another word that is almost as overworked today as *thrill*. It was originally a northern dialect word, being a corruption of *grammar*, the meaning of which was "learning", in which sense it is still used in "grammar school". Its meaning changed as the result of the superstition that confused learning with magic; it came to mean a spell. This is the meaning it had when Walter Scott found it and used it in his novels. Because of its romantic associations it gradually took on the meaning of "enchanting spell" and then "alluring charm". Its present meaning is a special sense of this last one.

Some words betray the prejudices of their makers. Learning used to be confined to the cities, and the bias of city-dwellers is clearly seen in such words as *civilized, polite, urbane*, all used when we wish to speak well of people's manners, and all derived from words meaning or to do with *city*. Thus *civilized* comes from the Latin *civis* (a member of a city, a citizen); *polite* from the Greek *polis* (a city); and *urbane* from the Latin *urbs* (a city). On the other hand, if we want to speak unfavourably of people we use adjectives that have to do with life in the country, such as *boorish, villainous, barbarian*. Of these, *boorish* comes from *bur*, meaning a farmer (*neighbour =* *nigh-bur* = a near farmer = a near dweller) and *villainous* comes *villanus*, meaning a farm servant. The word *barbarian* shows an even more contemptuous attitude. It comes from the Latin *barbarus*, which was formed in imitation of the speech of foreign tribes living in the wild country areas north of Rome.

To an arrogant Roman who did not try to understand foreign languages (including perhaps Anglo-Saxon !) any foreign tongue was an unintelligible babble—a "bar-bar".

Another word connected with the habits of people is *tawdry*, which came into use in the sixteenth century. It derives from the name of St Audrey (a corruption of Etheldreda), the patron saint of finery. A fair in her honour was held on 17th October of each year, but the idea was much abused and lace and trinkets of poor quality were sold to the unsuspecting, till in time St Audrey's fair became identified with cheap and trumpery objects. Such objects were then called tawdry, a shortened form of St Audrey, in which the *t* has been wrongly attached to "Audrey".

The verb *to burke* also derives from the name of a person, but its history is even grimmer. Burke was hanged in 1829 for suffocating people in order to sell their bodies to the medical schools. Hence a discussion or inquiry that is burked has been metaphorically smothered.

These are only a few of the sidelights thrown on the development of society as a result of the study of words. Etymology may be a science but it is a very human one.

EXERCISES

A. Find from the italicized list an adjective of classical origin to match each of the following from Old English. They will be more or less synonymous.

1. wordy	4. hellish	7. motherly	10. slow
2. lawful	5. brotherly	8. worldly	11. side
3. praiseworthy	6. salty	9. lofty	12. childish

infernal	*fraternal*	*saline*	*mundane*
verbose	*legal*	*laudable*	*elevated*
maternal	*lateral*	*puerile*	*dilatory*

B. With which of these Old English nouns does each of the italicized adjectives of Latin origin correspond?

1. sea	4. star	7. night	10. horse
2. water	5. spring	8. blood	11. hand
3. eye	6. child	9. body	12. eagle

aquatic	*puerile*	*vernal*	*ocular*
stellar	*corporeal*	*aquiline*	*nocturnal*
equine	*marine*	*manual*	*sanguinary*

C. The following adjectives, which derive from proper names, are used to denote the characteristics in the italicized list below. Refer to a good dictionary or encyclopedia, then pair each adjective with its characteristic. Begin: 1. Quixotic means to be foolishly chivalrous, with impossibly high ideals.

1. Quixotic 3. Rabelaisian 5. Saturnine 7. Delphic
2. Machiavellian 4. Chauvinistic 6. Vandalic 8. Tartuffian

(a) *obscure or ambiguous*, (b) *wilfully destructive*, (c) *foolishly chivalrous, with impossibly high ideals*, (d) *a religious hypocrite*, (e) *aggressively patriotic*, (f) *coarsely humorous*, (g) *gloomy and morose*, (h) *unscrupulous in statecraft*.

D. Now try to find out the proper names from which the adjectives in C. derive, and write short descriptions of the originals. For example : 1. Quixotic derives from Don Quixote, the hero of a book of the same name by the Spanish writer Miguel de Cervantes. The book was intended to ridicule the romances of chivalry that were very popular at the time.

E. Here are some stories showing how certain words originated. Find the right word to fill each blank.

1. A signal fire kindled on the top of a hill was called a *bēacan* by the Anglo-Saxons. From this is derived not only *beacon* but also —, which means to signal by a gesture of the hand.

2. The officer who bears the staff before a bishop owes his name to the Latin *virga*, a twig. The title of — refers also to the official who acts as usher in a church.

3. Early in the eighteenth century Sir William Gage, a gentleman of Norfolk, introduced from France a roundish green plum of fine flavour, which was named — after him.

4. The writing material of the ancients was prepared from the stems of a plant called the papyrus. During the second century B.C. there was introduced in the city of Pergamum, in the Mysia district of Asia Minor, the first substitute for papyrus. It was made from the skins of sheep and goats, and from the place of its origin (now known as Bergama) it derives the name — by which it is still known.

5. From the Latin word *vermis* (a worm) the Italians have formed a plural diminutive, meaning "little worms", to describe a popular food made from wheat. We too use — for soups and puddings.

USING a DICTIONARY

10

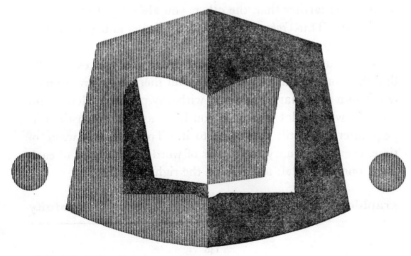

USING A DICTIONARY

The words of a dictionary are arranged in alphabetical order. To use one, you must therefore be able to follow an alphabetical arrangement with ease and rapidity. Remember that when two words begin with the same letter you arrange them according to the second letter of each. Thus *able* comes before *argue* because *b* comes before *r*. If the second letter of each word is the same you arrange them according to the third letter, and if the third letter is the same in each you arrange them according to the fourth; and so on. Hence *ability* comes before *able* because *i* comes before *l*. *Able*, however, comes before *ably* because *e* comes before *y*.

There is one other thing you need to know about alphabetical order: if two words have exactly the same letters, but one goes on farther than the other, you always put the shorter word first. Thus *Johns* comes before *Johnson*, and *assist* comes before *assistance*.

If you understand alphabetical order you can eventually find the word you are looking for. But there are a great many words in a dictionary beginning with any particular letter and you will waste a lot of time if you have to look down the list, page after page, till you come to it. To avoid this waste of time, every dictionary has a pair of words at the head of each page, one on the left and one on the right, like this:

graphically   527   **gratuity**

These are called guide words. They guide us in quickly finding the word we want. The one on the left tells us the first word dealt with on that page, and the one on the right tells us the last word dealt with. By their help we can tell at a glance whether the word we want is on that page ; we do not have to read down the whole page.

If we are looking for the word *grapple*, for example, we open the dictionary at the *g* part and then quickly turn over the pages, glancing at the guide words till we see the pair between which our word comes. In the *Concise Oxford Dictionary* this will be on page 527 between *graphically* and *gratuity*. We then read down the page till we come to the word *grapple* in its correct alphabetical order. This is the entry we find :

> **grăp′ple,** n., & v.t. and i. **1.** Clutching-instrument, grapnel. **2.** Hold or grip (as) of wrestlers, close contest. **3.** vb. Seize, fasten, (as) with grapnel ; take hold of, grip, with the hands, come to close quarters with, contend *with*, *together*, or abs., in close fight, battle *with* ; ∼ *with*, try to overcome, accomplish, or deal with. [vb f. n. in first sense ; second sense of n. f. vb ; n. f. OF dim. of *grape* hook]

What information, then, does such an entry give us ? First it gives us the correct spelling. Then it tells us that the word is stressed on the first syllable. The pronunciation is normal, the *a* being pronounced like *a* in *rack*. We know this because if it had been in any way unusual it would have been translated into simple phonetics as set out at the beginning of this dictionary. When the word is normal its pronunciation is merely indicated by marks over the vowels, as explained at the beginning of the dictionary.

The first abbreviations tell us that it can be used as a noun and as a transitive and intransitive verb. Then we have the three meanings of the word. The first two are obviously nouns, and the third is stated to be a verb. At the end of the third meaning, which is evidently the most common, we are given an example of an expression in which it is used—*to grapple with*—together with its meaning.

Finally, in square brackets, we are told about the word's etymology. The verb derives from the noun used in the first sense—a clutching-instrument. Then from the verb the noun in the second sense was developed. The original noun came from Old French *grape*, meaning a hook, and was a diminutive form of this.

Where alternative spellings, pronunciation or stress are given in the dictionary, it is usually the first one that is preferred by the compiler, e.g. *whiz, whizz*.

A good dictionary, then, will tell us everything we need to know about a word. But it would be foolish to suppose that you can use one without practice. Working through *Word Perfect* will help you to understand what to look for and how to interpret it when you have found it; but only practice will allow you to do this with any ease. Moreover, it is necessary to know the peculiarities of the particular dictionary you are using, for each one is different. No two dictionaries, unfortunately, indicate the stress, pronunciation, meanings and derivations in quite the same way, and they all use slightly different abbreviations. It is therefore essential to read the introduction of your dictionary carefully, to find out how these matters are dealt with. The dozen pages of introduction to the *Concise Oxford Dictionary*, for example, are an education in themselves, and would be well worth reading even if you never had occasion to use the dictionary.

EXERCISES

A. Here is an alphabetical list : *savoury, scone, shortbread, skate, sole, soup, sugar, syrup.* Rewrite the list, adding to it in their right places the following : *semolina, sandwich, sauce, sausage, sardines, sweetbreads, sirloin, sponge, strawberries.*

B. Arrange these names as you would expect to find them in a school register : *Patteson, Atkinson, Baker, Robinson, Williams, Browning, Smith, Smythe, Brown, Thomas, Thompson, Pattison, Wrigley, Hoover, Wright, Hooper, Hopkins, Barnet, Hopkinson.*

C. Which five of the following words would be found on page 527 of the *Concise Oxford Dictionary* ?

grasp	grandiose	gratitude	grass	grub
grapple	gross	graphite	grant	group

D. Here are the guide words on four different pages of the *Concise Oxford Dictionary* :

compilation	243	**compose**
composer	244	**compressible**
compression	245	**conceive**
condemn	248	**conduct**

On which page does each of the following words appear ?

1. compromise   4. condescend   7. comprehensible
2. compositor   5. complementary   8. condolatory
3. conceivable   6. complicity   9. compunction

E. Look up the word *canter* in any two dictionaries and note the differences in the information given.

F. The phonetic scheme used in the *Concise Oxford Dictionary* is :

Consonants

  b ; *ch* (chin) ; *d* ; *dh* (*dhe* = the) ; *g* (go) ; *h* ; *j* ; *k* ; *l* ; *m* ;
  n ; *ng* (sing) ; *ngg* (finger) ; *p* ; *r* ; *s* (sip) ; *sh* (ship) ; *t* ;
  th (thin) ; *v* ; *w* ; *z* ; *zh* (*vizhn* = vision)

Vowels

  ā, ē, ī, ō, ū, ōō (mate, mete, mite, mote, mute, moot)
  ă, ĕ, ĭ, ŏ, ŭ, ŏŏ (rack, reck, rick, rock, ruck, rook)
  ār, ēr, īr, ōr, ūr (mare, mere, mire, more, mure)
  âr, êr, ôr (part, pert, port)
  ah, aw, oi, oor, ou, our (bah, bawl, boil, boor, brow, bower)

Here are some words translated into these phonetic symbols.
(a) State what word each represents. (b) Translate each word
into international phonetic symbols (see page 62).

  1. kŭzn   3. āk   5. fōk'sl   7. vū
  2. kōrs   4. drahft 6. bō   8. krōōshl

G. By consulting a good dictionary give each of these words the
number of meanings indicated in brackets ; indicate the stress
and state the part of speech in each case.

  1. invalid (3)   4. race (4)   7. shock (5)
  2. intimate (3)   5. strike (4) 8. post (6)
  3. match (3)   6. order (4)   9. deal (5)

H. Again by consulting a dictionary, explain the different
meanings of the word *address* as used in these sentences :

  1. Begin the address half-way down the envelope.
  2. It is important to address your letters correctly.
  3. The address he delivered on Speech Day gave us food
      for thought.
  4. The headmaster began to address the assembled school.
  5. Jim paid his addresses to the young actress without avail,
      as she was not attracted to him.

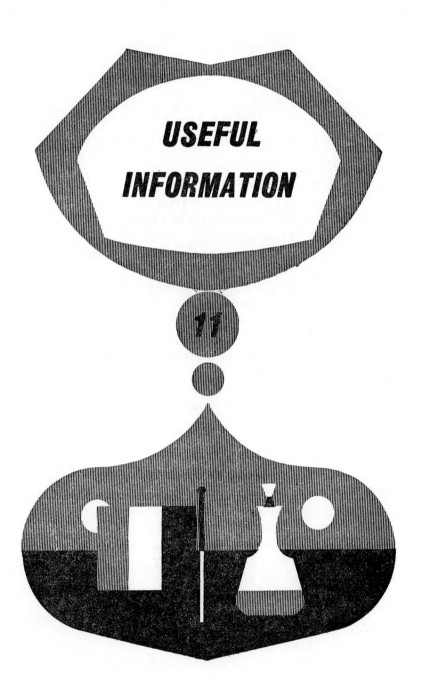

USEFUL

INFORMATION

11

USEFUL INFORMATION

(i) *Abbreviations*

A.A.A.   Amateur Athletic Association

A.C.E.   Advisory Centre for Education

A.D.   (*Anno Domini*) in the year of our Lord

A.D.C.   Aide-de-Camp

ad lib.   (*ad libitum*) at pleasure; as much as you wish

a.m.   (*ante meridiem*) before noon

A.R.A.   Associate of the Royal Academy

A.T.C.   Air Training Corps

A.T.V.   Associated Television Ltd.

B.M.A.   British Medical Association

B.O.A.C.   British Overseas Airways Corporation

B.S.A.   Birmingham Small Arms

Cantab.   (*Cantabrigiensis*) of Cambridge University

C.B.E.   Commander of the Order of the British Empire

cf.   (*confer, conferatur*) compare

C.H.   Companion of Honour

C.I.D.   Criminal Investigation Department

C.M.S.   Church Missionary Society

Co.   Company; County

Coy.   Company (usually military)

C.S.M.   Company Sergeant-Major

C.W.S.   Co-operative Wholesale Society

D.F.C.   Distinguished Flying Cross

D.H.S.S.   Department of Health and Social Security

do.   (*ditto*) the same

D.S.O.   Distinguished Service Order

D.V. (*Deo volente*) God willing
e.g. (*exempli gratia*) for example
et seq. (*et sequentes*) and the following
E.E.C. European Economic Community
Fahr. Fahrenheit (thermometer)
F.R.C.S. Fellow of the Royal College of Surgeons
F.R.S. Fellow of the Royal Society
G.M.T. Greenwich Mean Time
G.O.C. General Officer Commanding
G.P. General Practitioner
H.M.I. Her Majesty's Inspector (of Schools)
H.M.S.O. Her Majesty's Stationery Office
Hon. Sec. Honorary Secretary
ib. (*ibidem*) in the same place
i.e. (*id est*) that is
I.L.O. International Labour Organization
incog. (*incognitus*, unknown) incognito, e.g. travelling under
    an assumed name
I.O.W. Isle of Wight
I.R.A. Irish Republican Army
I.T.A. Independent Television Authority
J.P. Justice of the Peace
K.C.B. Knight Commander of the Order of the Bath
K.G. Knight of the Order of the Garter
K.G.C. Knight Grand Cross
lb. (*libra*) a pound in weight
L.C.M. Lowest Common Multiple
LL.B. (*Legum Baccalaureus*) Bachelor of Laws
LL.D. (*Legum Doctor*) Doctor of Laws
L.T.E. London Transport Executive
M.B. (*Medicinae Baccalaureus*) Bachelor of Medicine
M.B.E. Member of the Order of the British Empire
M.C. Master of Ceremonies; Military Cross
M.C.C. Marylebone Cricket Club

M.D. (*Medicinae Doctor*) Doctor of Medicine; Mental defective

memo (plural *memos*) memorandum (plural *memoranda*)

Messrs. (*Messieurs*) plural of *Mr*

M.M. Military Medal

M.O.H. Medical Officer of Health

M.R.C.P. Member of the Royal College of Physicians

M.R.C.S. Member of the Royal College of Surgeons

MS (plural *MSS*) (*manuscriptum*) manuscript

Mus.B., Mus.Bac. (*Musicae Baccalaureus*) Bachelor of Music

N.A.A.F.I. (Naafi) Navy, Army and Air Force Institutes

N.A.T.O. (NATO) North Atlantic Treaty Organization

N.B. (*Nota bene*) Note well

N.C.B. National Coal Board

N.F.E.R. National Foundation for Educational Research

N.H.S. National Health Service

N.S.P.C.C. National Society for the Prevention of Cruelty to Children

N.S.W. New South Wales

N.U.T. National Union of Teachers

O.B.E. Officer of the Order of the British Empire

O.F.S. Orange Free State

O.M. Order of Merit

op. cit. (*opere citato*) in the work quoted

O.U.P. Oxford University Press

Oxon. Of Oxford University; Oxfordshire

P. & O. Peninsular and Oriental (Steam Navigation Co.)

P.A.Y.E. Pay As you Earn

per pro (*per procurationem*) on behalf of

P.G. Paying Guest

P.P.S. Parliamentary Private Secretary

pro tem. (*pro tempore*) for the time being

Pty. Proprietary (as used by Australian companies)

Q.C. Queen's Counsel

Q.E.D. (*Quod erat demonstrandum*) Which was to be proved

q.v. (*quod vide*) which see

R.A.F. Royal Air Force

R.D.C. Rural District Council

R.E.M.E. Royal Electrical and Mechanical Engineers

R.I.B.A. Royal Institute of British Architects

R.S.P.C.A. Royal Society for the Prevention of Cruelty to Animals

R.S.V.P. (*Répondez, s'il vous plaît*) Reply, if you please

s.a.e. Stamped addressed envelope

Salop Shropshire

S.J. (*Societas Jesu*) Society of Jesus (Jesuits)

S.O.S. (Save Our Souls) Distress signal

S.R.N. State Registered Nurse

T.T. teetotaller; tuberculin-tested; Tourist trophy

T.W.A. Trans-World Airlines

U.D.C. Urban District Council

U.N.C.T.A.D. United Nations Conference on Trade and Development

U.N.E.S.C.O. (UNESCO) United Nations Educational, Scientific and Cultural Organization

U.S.S.R. Union of Soviet Socialist Republics

V.H.F. Very High Frequency

viz. (*videlicet*), namely (and so pronounced; one should not say 'viz.'

W.H.O. World Health Organization

W.P.B. Waste-paper basket

W.V.S. Women's Voluntary Services

Y.H.A. Youth Hostels Association

(ii) *Similes*

as bitter as gall

as black as sin

as bold as brass

as brown as a berry

as busy as a bee

as clean as a new pin

as clear as crystal

as cold as charity

as cool as a cucumber

as cross as two sticks

as cunning as a fox

as dead as mutton

as deaf as a post

as dry as a bone

as dull as ditchwater

as easy as winking

as fast as a deer

as firm as a rock

as fit as a fiddle

as flat as a pancake

as fresh as paint

as frisky as a two-year-old

as fussy as an old hen

as gentle as a lamb

as good as gold

as happy as a sandboy

as hard as nails

as hot as a furnace

as hungry as a hunter

as industrious as a beaver

as keen as mustard

as large as life

as like as two peas

as mad as a hatter

as meek as a lamb

as merry as a cricket

as obstinate as a mule

as old as Methuselah

as pale as death

as patient as Job

as plain as a pikestaff

as playful as a kitten

as pleased as Punch

as poor as a church mouse

as proud as a peacock

as quiet as a mouse

as red as a beetroot

as regular as a clock

as right as ninepence

as round as a barrel

as safe as houses

as silent as the grave

as slippery as an eel

as smooth as velvet

as sober as a judge

as soft as silk

as sound as a bell

as sour as vinegar

as stiff as a poker

as straight as a ramrod

as strong as an ox

as sturdy as an oak

as sure-footed as a goat

as sweet as a nut

as tenacious as a bulldog
as thick as thieves
as thin as a rake
as timid as a mouse
as tough as leather
as true as steel
as warm as toast
as weak as water
as white as a sheet
as wise as an owl

like a bull in a china shop
like a cat on hot bricks
like a fish out of water
like a house on fire
like a red rag to a bull
like hot cakes (sold fast)
like sardines (crowded)
like the curate's egg (excellent in parts)
like water off a duck's back
like wildfire

(iii) *Collective Nouns*

an anthology of poems
an assembly of statesmen
the audience in a theatre
a batch of cakes
a bench of magistrates
a bevy of quails
a board of directors
a bouquet of flowers
a brood of chicks
a chattering of starlings
a choir of singers
a clump of trees
a cluster of stars
a clutch of eggs
a colony of gulls
a company of actors
a compendium of games
a congregation of worshippers
a covey of partridges
the crew of a ship or aircraft

a drove of cattle
a fleet of ships or taxis
a flight of aircraft
a flock of sheep or birds
a gaggle of geese
a galaxy of beautiful women
a gang of navvies
a gathering of clans
a hail of bullets
a hand of bananas (each a "finger")
a herd of buffaloes
a horde of savages
a host of angels
the jury in a court of justice
a library of books
a litter of pups or piglets
a mob of rioters
a muster of peacocks
a nest of machine-guns

an orchard of fruit-trees
an outfit of clothes
a pack of wolves
a peal of bells
a plague of locusts
a posse of policemen
a pride of lions
a rope of pearls
a school of whales or porpoises
a set of golf clubs

a sheaf of papers
a shoal of herring
a skein of wild geese in flight
a staff of teachers
a stud of horses
a suite of furniture
a swarm of bees
a team of oxen
a tribe of Zulus
a troop of monkeys
a troupe of dancers

(iv) *Noises*

the babble of a stream
the beat of a drum
the blare of a trumpet
the blast of an explosion
the bubbling of a stream
the buzz of conversation
the chattering of a brook
the chime of a clock
the chinking of coins
the chug of an engine
the clang of a bell
the clanking of chains
the clatter of hoofs
the click of a latch
the crack of a whip
the crackle of a fire
the creak of floorboards
the crinkle of tin-foil
the fizz of lemonade
the grinding of brakes

the gurgle of a waste-pipe
the hiss of steam
the hoot of a horn
the howling of the wind
the hubbub of many voices
the hum of a sewing-machine
the jangle of bells out of tune
the jingle of coins
the lapping of sea waves
the murmur of a stream
the patter of little feet
the pealing of church bells
the ping of a travelling bullet
the pitter-patter of raindrops
the popping of corks
the purr of a Rolls Royce
the rasp of a file
the rattle of crockery
the ring of a coin
the roar of a furnace

the rumble of a train
the rustle of silk
the rustling of leaves
the scrape of a violin bow
the screeching of brakes
the shriek of a circular saw
the shuffling of feet
the sighing of the wind
the sizzling of frying bacon
the slam of a door
the sputter of green wood on a fire

the susurration of car tyres
the swish of skirts
the throb of an engine
the thunder of galloping hoofs
the tick of a clock
the tinkling of a small bell
the toot of a horn
the twang of a bow
the wail of a siren
the whir of a propeller
the zoom of an aircraft as it climbs suddenly

(v) *Utterances and Movements*

an ape gibbers and swings
a bear growls and lumbers
a bee buzzes and ranges
a bull bellows and charges
a cat purrs and steals (moves quietly)
a cock crows and struts
a deer bells and bounds
a dog barks and runs
a donkey brays and trots
a duck quacks and waddles
an eagle screams and swoops
an elephant trumpets and ambles
a frog croaks and leaps
a horse neighs and gallops
a hound bays and bounds
a hyena howls and prowls
a lamb bleats and frisks

a lark sings and soars
a lion roars and prowls
a monkey chatters and climbs
a mouse squeaks and scampers
an owl hoots and flits
a parrot screeches and flits
a pig grunts and trots
a pigeon coos and flutters
a rabbit squeals and leaps
a seagull screams and glides
a serpent hisses and glides
a sparrow chirps and hops
a swallow twitters and dives
a turkey gobbles and struts
a wolf howls and lopes
a woodpecker yaffles and climbs
a wren warbles and hops

(vi) *Some Classifications*

Animate things: men, trees, plants, dogs, birds, vegetables, snakes

Inanimate things: desk, clothes, metals, knives, cement, crockery

Cutlery: knives, forks, spoons, carvers, ladles

Reptiles: snakes, lizards, crocodiles, turtles, tortoises

Gems: emeralds, pearls, diamonds, rubies, sapphires

Cereals: maize, wheat, rye, oats, rice, barley, millet

Manual workers: farmer, navvy, labourer, sweep, porter, miner

Sedentary workers: clerk, teacher, secretary, typist, tailor, solicitor

Wood-wind instruments: flute, clarinet, oboe, bassoon

Reference books: dictionary, encyclopedia, directory, atlas

Sentiments: love, jealousy, hatred, envy, admiration

(vii) *Homonyms*

The word *homonym* is made up of the Greek *homo* (same) and *onoma* (name). Homonyms are therefore words spelt alike but meaning different things. They may be words that derive from the same source, but whose meanings have diverged. An example of this type is *box* meaning a tree and *box* meaning a container. Or they may come from different sources and yet happen to be spelt alike and even pronounced alike. An example of this type is *port* meaning a wine and deriving from the name of its origin, Oporto, and *port* meaning a harbour and derived from the Latin *portus* (harbour). There are also three other homonyms: *port* meaning an opening in a ship, from the Latin *porta* (a door); *port* meaning bearing, from *portare* (to carry); and *port* meaning the left side of a ship, from an unknown source.

Homonyms must be spelt alike, though they need not be pronounced alike. Thus *bow* meaning a weapon to shoot arrows, and *bow* meaning to bend are homonyms. But words pronounced alike and spelt differently are not, strictly speaking, homonyms; they are homophones.

Here is a short list of homonyms, with meanings distinguished:

bank, sloping ground	*leaves*, plural of leaf
bank, place where money is kept	*leaves*, departs
bark, covering of tree trunks	*like*, similar to
bark, cry of a dog	*like*, to think well of
bear, animal	*pole*, long piece of wood
bear, to carry	*pole*, extremity of an axis
charger, large flat dish	*shelves*, plural of shelf
charger, officer's horse	*shelves*, slopes gently
corn, grain	*stole*, vestment
corn, horny place on foot	*stole*, past tense of *steal*
fair, market	*tick*, sound made by clock
fair, beautiful; blond	*tick*, parasitic insect
fair, satisfactory; reasonable	*tick*, mattress cover
heel, lean of a ship	*tick*, credit
heel, rear part of foot	*till*, to cultivate the soil
lead, metal	*till*, up to the time of
lead, to guide	*till*, drawer for money

(viii) *Homophones*

The word *homophone* comes from the Greek *homo* (same) and *phōnē* (sound). Homophones are therefore words pronounced alike but having different spelling and meaning or usage. Sometimes they derive from the same source, as do *practice* (noun) and *practise* (verb). More frequently they derive from different sources, as do *maize* (corn) and *maze* (labyrinth). But in either case the different spelling is explained by the fact that English is not wholly phonetic, often using different letters to represent the same sound.

On the next page is a short list of homophones.

air, atmosphere	*him*, objective case of *he*
heir, inheritor	*hymn*, song of praise
all, entire	*knead*, to work flour into dough
awl, tool	*need*, want
bail, security given	*meat*, flesh used as food
bale, bundle of goods	*meet*, to encounter
bald, hairless	*reek*, smoke
bawled, shouted	*wreak*, to revenge
bare, uncovered	*right*, correct
bear, animal; to carry	*rite*, solemn ceremony
boy, male child	*write*, to set down on paper
buoy, anchored float	*rye*, kind of grain
braid, to plait together	*wry*, twisted
brayed, cried like an ass	*sew*, to use needle and cotton
coat, garment	*so*, therefore
cote, shed or inclosure	*sow*, to plant seeds
fair, market	*son*, male offspring
fare, price paid for journey	*sun*, heavenly body
frays, fights	*steal*, to purloin
phrase, part of a sentence	*steel*, metal
gilt, covered with thin gold	*wait*, to stay for something
guilt, wickedness	*weight*, heaviness

(ix) *Puns*

It is because it has so many homonyms and homophones that the English language lends itself to puns more than most languages. A pun may be defined as a (usually) humorous play on words having a similar sound but different meanings. Let us examine some different types of pun.

Is life worth living? It depends upon the liver. Here the play is upon the homonyms *liver*, meaning a glandular organ, and *liver*, meaning one who lives. It could be either *liver* that is meant; and therein lies the humour.

The drunkard felt quite sure he wanted a bier to take him to his funeral. This time it is a play upon the homophones *beer* and *bier*. The humour falls flat in print. A pun based upon homophones is better heard, not seen.

In everyday conversation most of our puns are based on neither homophones or homonyms, but on words that have to be stretched to be made to sound similar. This is a poor type of pun that passes muster only in quick exchanges. Such a pun might be made if someone lost his car and his friend quickly said : "That is very car(e)less of you".

(x) *Some Containers and Contents*

barrel	beer	fob	watch
brief-case	documents	hamper	picnic
bunker	coal	hangar	aircraft
butt	rainwater	holster	pistol
caddy	tea	keg	rum
carafe	wine	phial	medicine
carton	large ice cream	portmanteau	clothing
cask	cider	punnet	strawberries
compact	face powder	reticule	shopping
drum	oil	scabbard	sword
ewer	water	urn	ashes of the dead

(xi) *Countries*

Country	Adjective	Language	Monetary Unit
Argentina	Argentine	Spanish	peso
Australia	Australian	English	Australian pound
Belgium	Belgian	Flemish and French	Belgian franc
Brazil	Brazilian	Portuguese	cruzeiro
Chile	Chilean	Spanish	peso
China	Chinese	Chinese	dollar

(xi) *Countries—contd.*

Country	Adjective	Language	Monetary Unit
Czechoslovakia	Czechoslovakian	Czech and Slovak	koruna
Denmark	Danish	Danish	krone
Egypt	Egyptian	Arabic	Egyptian pound
Eire	Irish	English	Irish pound
Finland	Finnish	Finnish	markka
Ghana	Ghanaian	English	Ghana pound
Greece	Greek	Greek	drachma
Greenland	Greenlandic	Danish and Eskimo	that of Denmark
Hungary	Hungarian	Magyar (or Hungarian)	forint
Iceland	Icelandic	Icelandic	króna
India	Indian	Hindi and English	rupee
Israel	Israeli	Hebrew	Israeli pound
Jamaica	Jamaican	English	pound
Mexico	Mexican	Spanish	peso
Netherlands	Dutch	Dutch	guilder or florin
Nigeria	Nigerian	English	West African shilling
Norway	Norwegian	Norwegian and Lappish	króne
Portugal	Portuguese	Portuguese	escudo
Russia	Russian	Russian	rouble
Sweden	Swedish	Swedish	krona
Switzerland	Swiss	German and French	franc
Turkey	Turkish	Turkish	lira
United States	American	English	dollar
Yugoslavia	Yugoslavian	Serbo-Croat-Slovene	dinar

(xii) *Library Classification*

The commonest way of classifying books in a library is by the Dewey Decimal Classification. This divides knowledge into nine main classes, with a tenth class to cover books so general that they do not belong to any one of the main classes. Each main class is separated into 10 divisions, and each division into 10 sections, and then by decimals each section may be separated into smaller sections. Thus 512 means class 5 (Natural Science), division 1 (Mathematics), section 2 (Algebra). All books on algebra will therefore be numbered 512. In a very large library the 512 section may be further divided by the decimal point, e.g. 512·8 (Higher Algebra). Below are the main classes and sample divisions or sections :

000 GENERAL WORKS
  010 Bibliography
  070 Journalism

100 PHILOSOPHY
  150 Psychology
  160 Logic
  190 Modern Philosophers

200 RELIGION
  220 The Christian Bible
  270 Church History
  294 Buddhism
  297 The Moslem Faith

300 SOCIOLOGY
  330 Economics
  370 Education
  383 Postage Stamps
  390 Customs
  394 Christmas Customs

400 PHILOLOGY
  420 English Language
  423 English Dictionaries
  425 English Grammar
  440 French Language
  491·62 Irish Language
  491·7 Russian Language

500 NATURAL SCIENCE
  511 Arithmetic
  520 Astronomy
  530 Physics
  535 Optics
  570 Biology

600 USEFUL ARTS
  608 Inventions
  629·2 Motor Vehicles
  641·5 Cookery
  654 Telegraphy

700 FINE ARTS
  720 Architecture
  746 Tapestry
  770 Photography
  780 Music

800 LITERATURE
  810 American
  820 English
  822 English Drama
  823 English Fiction
  850 Italian

900 HISTORY
  916 Travel in Asia
  994 Australian History

EXERCISES

A. The English language is spoken and written in both the United Kingdom and the U.S.A., but with certain minor differences. Among these are differences of vocabulary. For example, a concreted path alongside a street is called a *pavement* in British English and a *sidewalk* in American English. The American *pavement* is our *roadway*. Now pair with each of these British nouns its equivalent American noun:

1. motor-car	7. petrol	cracker	candies
2. sweets	8. full stop	faucet	gas
3. biscuit	9. braces	period	truck
4. chemist's	10. lorry	suspenders	vest
5. tap	11. holiday	automobile	drug-store
6. ironmongery	12. waistcoat	vacation	hardware

B. Two homonyms have been used in each of the following sentences. Explain their difference in meaning.

1. As the wind began to blow, I felt a blow on the head.
2. Mrs Smith rubbed off the scales and then weighed the fish on her kitchen scales
3. A row of boys were waiting to go for a row in the boat.
4. He rode his bay horse across the sandy bay.
5. Since he struck it against the tender of the engine, his head has felt very tender.

C. Give three different meanings for each of these words:
    1. fine   2. form   3. sole   4. deal   5. bear

D. Distinguish the meanings of these homophones:

1. faint and feint	5. mote and moat	9. signet and cygnet
2. vale and veil	6. preys and praise	10. choler and collar
3. wave and waive	7. creek and creak	11. laps and lapse
4. base and bass	8. naval and navel	12. metal and mettle

E. The italicized words are homophones. Use each to complete one of the sentences below.

stationery	dependent	principle	muscle
stationary	dependant	principal	mussel
hoard	compliment	sucker	serial
horde	complement	succour	cereal

1. Rice is the commonest — grown in Ceylon.
2. The miser kept his — of gold in a thick stocking.
3. Children are — upon their parents for their support.
4. Coming from the Latin *succurro* (I run to), — means to go to someone else's assistance.
5. As all the sailors had reported for duty, the ship was able to go to sea with her full —.
6. The boy kept perfectly still, not moving a —.
7. The missionaries were suddenly attacked by a — of savages.
8. He paid me the — of recommending me for promotion.
9. The car did not move as expected, but remained —.
10. Peter was reading the final instalment of an exciting —.
11. She bought a box of — and wrote to all her friends.
12. A — is a bivalve mollusc.
13. In America a — is a person who is very easily deceived.
14. Not being able to fend for himself, the old man was a — of the rich landowner.
15. One should make it a — never to bathe immediately after a heavy meal.
16. When at the seaside the — thing to avoid is bathing immediately after a heavy meal.

F. Try to explain how the pun occurs in this :

> Ben Battle was a soldier bold,
> And used to war's alarms :
> But a cannon-ball took off his legs,
> So he laid down his arms !
>
> THOMAS HOOD

G. What is the collective noun that names a collection of:

1.	cows	3.	wolves	5.	fruit-trees	7.	porpoises
2.	sheep	4.	furniture	6.	directors	8.	bananas

H. Choose the correct word to complete these sentences:

1. Gills and fins are associated with (measures, cats, fish, birds).
2. Necks and corks are associated with (people, bottles, trees).
3. Staves and hoops are associated with (bottles, barrels, music).
4. Writing and clasping are associated with (books, knives, pens, hands).
5. Keys and pedals are associated with (doors, cycles, pianos, rooms).

I. Divide each of the lists below into two sub-lists of seven, using these classifications: 1 (a) manual workers, (b) sedentary workers; 2 (a) salt-water fish, (b) fresh-water fish; 3 (a) wind instruments, (b) stringed instruments. Name the "odd man out" in each main list and explain why.

1. accountant, author, banker, bargee, carpenter, commercial artist, electrician, magistrate, mason, pensioner, playwright, plumber, steeple-jack, stoker, underwriter
2. carp, cod, chub, goldfish, herring, mackerel, pike, plaice, salmon, sardine, sole, tench, trout, turbot, whale
3. bugle, dulcimer, fife, flageolet, flute, guitar, harp, lute, lyre, mandolin, saxophone, tambourine, trumpet, tuba, violin

J. Say which you would consult to find:

1.	what happened yesterday	an atlas
2.	the pronunciation of a word	a directory
3.	the position of Bermuda	today's newspaper
4.	facts on many different subjects	a timetable
5.	a family photograph	a dictionary
6.	the take-off time of an airliner	an album
7.	the address of a friend	an encyclopedia

K. Give these abbreviations in full:

1. G.P.O.   3. N.B.   5. J.P.   7. e.g.   9. i.e.
2. B.B.C.   4. C.W.S.   6. I.L.O.   8. viz.   10. et seq.

L. Write this list of capital cities in alphabetical order:

Budapest	Lagos	Bucharest	Buenos Aires
Delhi	Brussels	Copenhagen	Rio de Janeiro
Ottawa	Colombo	Prague	Karachi
Canberra	Ankara	Sofia	Amsterdam
Accra	Cairo	Stockholm	Washington

M. State which of the cities named in the box is the capital of each of these countries:

1. Rumania   6. Pakistan   11. Ghana   16. Hungary
2. Czechoslovakia 7. Argentina 12. India   17. Australia
3. United States 8. Holland   13. Nigeria   18. Turkey
4. Bulgaria   9. Sweden   14. Belgium   19. Egypt
5. Denmark   10. Brazil   15. Sri Lanka 20. Canada

N. Give its capital to each country below. If you do this correctly, the capital cities will be in alphabetical order.

1. Ethiopia   11. Tibet   Kuala Lumpur   Athens
2. Greece   12. Peru   Helsinki   Lima
3. Yugoslavia   13. Portugal   Tirana   Santiago
4. Switzerland 14. Kenya   Lhasa   Djakarta
5. Venezuela   15. Norway   Kabul   Berne
6. Indonesia   16. Burma   Rangoon   Lisbon
7. Finland   17. Chile   Kuching   Caracas
8. Afghanistan 18. Albania   Addis Ababa   Belgrade
9. Sarawak   19. Libya   Tripoli   Wellington
10. Malaya   20. New Zealand Nairobi   Oslo

O. Write the five counties that are in: (1) Scotland, (2) Wales, (3) England, (4) Northern Ireland.

Merionethshire	Hampshire	Midlothian	Fermanagh
Brecknockshire	Berkshire	Caithness	Antrim
Montgomeryshire	Shropshire	Berwickshire	Tyrone
Anglesey	Cheshire	East Lothian	Londonderry
Flintshire	Buckinghamshire	Argyllshire	Down

P. After each of these county towns write the name of the county to which it belongs. If you do this correctly, the counties, which are all in the box, will be in alphabetical order.

1. Beaumaris	8. Wick	15. Londonderry
2. Belfast	9. Chester	16. Dolgelley
3. Inveraray	10. Downpatrick	17. Edinburgh
4. Reading	11. Haddington	18. Welshpool
5. Duns	12. Enniskillen	19. Shrewsbury
6. Brecon	13. Mold	20. Omagh
7. Aylesbury	14. Winchester	

Q. Here are twenty more counties, thoroughly mixed this time. Write down the five that are in: (1) England, (2) Wales, (3) Scotland, (4) Northern Ireland.

Durham	Radnorshire	Tyrone	Pembrokeshire
Caernarvonshire	Devonshire	Banffshire	Cardiganshire
Fifeshire	Fermanagh	Suffolk	Gloucestershire
Perthshire	Lancashire	Inverness	Carmarthenshire
Armagh	Lanarkshire	Antrim	Londonderry

R. What are the adjectives used to describe these countries?

1. Denmark	3. Nigeria	5. Holland	7. Hungary
2. Canada	4. Ghana	6. Peru	8. Israel

SOME MISUSED WORDS

12

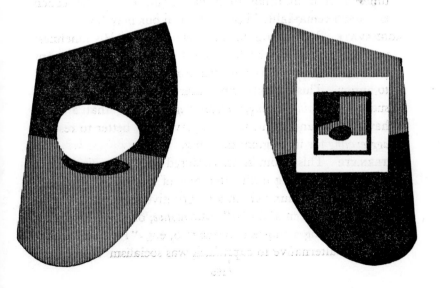

SECTION TWELVE

SOME MISUSED WORDS

ADMISSION This is sometimes confused with *admittance*. Generally the two words are interchangeable, but usage insists on "No admittance" for warning notices, and "The price of admission" for entrance money. Usage now also insists that when we admit something we make an *admission*.

ADVISE *To advise* means to give advice and should not be used when we mean simply to give information, since the verb *to inform* is already available for that.

AFFECT This is always a verb and means to influence. Though *effect* is usually a noun meaning result, it is sometimes a verb meaning to bring about, e.g. "The coach effected a remarkable improvement in our play".

AGGRAVATE This means to make worse, e.g. "His loneliness was aggravated by the loss of his parents". The present participle, however, is now commonly used in the sense of to annoy. This is a pity, since there are plenty of adjectives such as *annoying, vexing, exasperating, irritating* that already have this meaning and it would have been better to reserve *aggravating* for its original meaning.

ALTERNATE This is sometimes confused with *alternative*. *Alternate* means coming each after one of the other kind, e.g. "The alternate numbers in a consecutive series must be odd and even or even and odd". *Alternative*, on the other hand, means offering a choice between two, e.g. "He claimed that the only alternative to capitalism was socialism".

ALTERNATIVE   Strictly speaking, *alternative* should only be used when there is a choice between two. Thus, instead of saying, "We were faced with three alternatives", it would be better to say, "We were faced with three choices".

AMOUNT   This should be used of uncountable things but not of countable things. Thus it is correct to speak of "the amount of work", but instead of "the amount of mistakes" we should say, "The number of mistakes".

BESIDE   This means alongside, and should not be confused with *besides*, which means in addition to.

BETWEEN   We say that something is shared *between* two people, but we say that it is shared *among* more than two. This preposition is sometimes also confused with *after*, e.g. "The audience left the hall between each act". This is impossible since there is only a single act mentioned. There are two correct alternatives: "The audience left the hall between the acts", *or* "The audience left the hall after each act".

BOTH   This may not be used interchangeably with *each*. *Both* means two taken together, e.g. "Both these books cost a pound". (Total cost of the two is £1). *Each* means any number taken one at a time, e.g. "Each of these books costs a pound". (Total cost of the two is £2.)

CAN   The careful speaker makes a distinction between *can* and *may*. Strictly, the former means to be able to, and the latter means to have permission to. Thus if you want permission to go to the cinema you say, "May I go?" If you want to know if someone is able to swim you say, "Can you swim?"

CHRONIC   This adjective means having gone on for a long time; inveterate. It is therefore correct to speak of chronic rheumatism if it has lasted several months, even if it has not been very severe; but it is a misuse of the word to speak of a sudden chronic pain however severe it may be.

CLIENT This is thought to be a politer word than *customer*, and is euphemistically used when the latter would be better. It is an advantage to reserve *customer* for a person who pays for things he buys, and *client* for a person who pays for professional services. Two similar words are distinctive: *patient* meaning a person who receives medical services, and *guest* meaning a person who pays for hotel services.

CONTEMPTIBLE This adjective, which means deserving our contempt, must be clearly distinguished from *contemptuous*, which means showing contempt for someone else. We are therefore contemptuous of contemptible people.

CONTINUAL This is often confused with *continuous*. It is worth remembering that a continuous performance can be continually interrupted by fresh arrivals. *Continuous* means going on without a break, but *continual* means frequent.

DISINTERESTED A *disinterested* person is one who is impartial because without self-interest, and is therefore very different from an *uninterested* person, who is bored because lacking interest in or enthusiasm for something.

DUE TO This should not be confused with *owing to*: the two are not interchangeable. The former always introduces an adjectival phrase, and the latter an adverbial phrase, e.g. "I noticed a number of mistakes due to carelessness". "He failed the examination owing to lack of preparation".

FARTHER This has been so confused with *further* that usage now makes no distinction between the two. Some careful writers, however, like to reserve *farther* for greater distance, and *further* for more or additional, e.g. "A further point to consider is that he has travelled farther than us".

FEWER It is a useful distinction to use *fewer* for countable quantities and *less* for uncountable quantities, e.g. "There has been less rain today, so that fewer people are carrying umbrellas".

FORMER   This refers to the first of two things, and *latter* to the second of two things. Neither may be used when there are more than two things; we must then use *first* and *last*. In other words, *former* and *latter* are comparatives, while *first* and *last* are superlatives.

GET   This useful word is misused only in the sense that it is often used where a more exact verb would be clearer. *Have got* for "have" or "possess" is now considered good colloquial English, but it should be avoided in written English, except for dialogue.

GOURMAND   It is as well to know the difference between this and *gourmet*, since the former is a disparaging term and the latter a flattering one. The gourmand eats greedily, while the gourmet eats with discrimination.

HANGED   If the law is just, only criminals have ever been hanged. So long as the death sentence remains they will continue to be hanged; but they will never be hung. Pictures, however, are regularly hung.

LEARN   The misuse of *learn* for *teach* is a vulgarism much frowned on by the educated. Wrong: He learned me how to play chess. Right: He taught me how to play chess. Remember that *to learn* means to receive knowledge or to study, but *to teach* means to convey knowledge to someone else.

LEND   The use of *lend* for *borrow* is another vulgarism. We never lend from a person, but only to a person. We always borrow from him.

LIE   This verb is misused by confusion with *to lay*. There are three things to remember. First, *to lie* means to recline, while *to lay* means to place or put down an object, including an egg. Secondly, *to lie* is intransitive, while to lay is transitive. Thus you can lie somewhere, but you always lay something. Thirdly, the principal parts of *to lie* are lay, lying, lain; while those of *to lay* are laid, laying, laid. The matter is further complicated by the existence of *to lie* meaning to tell an untruth. The principal parts of this are lied, lying, lied. It will help to remember that you can lay down the law, but you cannot lay down on the job; if you are lazy you lie down on it instead.

LIKE   Strictly, this is a preposition, not a conjunction. The corresponding conjunction is *as*. This sentence is therefore incorrect: "I did it like he instructed me to". It should be corrected to: "I did it as he instructed me to". This distinction is usually maintained in literary English, though in colloquial English either passes.

LITERALLY   Since this adverb means taking the words in their literal or non-figurative sense, it is clearly a misuse of the word to say, "He was literally bursting with excitement". The direct opposite is intended: he was bursting figuratively, not literally. Intelligent people will resist this popular misuse of the word even in conversation.

MUTUAL   Careful writers will not confuse this adjective with *common*. To use *mutual* correctly there must be a relationship in which x is or does to y as y is or does to x. Thus we can say that our admiration is mutual if you admire me as much as I admire you. But if x has a friend z, and y also has the same friend z, z is not their mutual friend; he is merely their common friend.

OBSERVANCE   This will not be confused with *observation* if we remember that the former means attending to a duty or custom, while the latter means noticing or watching things.

PRACTICABLE   This means able to be put into practice or to be accomplished, while *practical* means adapted to actual conditions, not merely theoretical. It follows that a person can be practical, but he can never be practicable. An idea, however, can be both practical and practicable. It helps to remember that practical is the opposite of theoretical.

PRINCIPAL We shall avoid confusing this with *principle* if we remember that the former means chief and may be an adjective or a noun. Thus the principal member of a business and its principal are one and the same person. *Principle* means a rule of conduct, and is often used in the plural, e.g. "It was against his principles to mock the aged".

SCHOLAR *Pupil* and *scholar* are not interchangeable. A pupil is a child who goes to school to learn. A scholar is a learned person who devotes himself to original thought. As there is no other word to describe the latter, the word *scholar* is best reserved for that purpose.

SHALL The full difference between *shall* and *will* is summed up in this rule : for the simple future use *shall* in the first person and *will* in the second and third ; to express determination use *will* in the first person and *shall* in the second and third. "I will not go" means that I am determined not to go. "I shall not go" means that it is not my intention to go. This distinction in the first person is fast disappearing because neither Scotsmen nor Americans take any notice of it. The distinction is more important in the second and third persons. "You shall not do it" is a threat of your determination. "You will not do it" shows that you believe it is not his intention to do it.

TRANSPIRE This means to become known gradually or later on, and should not therefore be used where the simpler *happen* or *occur* could be used.

UNIQUE This is a word that can have no comparative or superlative. It means of which only one exists. A thing is therefore unique or not unique. It cannot be more unique or most unique. The purist would apply the same argument to *perfect, correct, round*. The difficulty can be overcome by saying that something is more nearly unique, perfect, etc.

W.P. BK. VIII—M

EXERCISES

Rewrite each of these sentences so as to avoid the misused word.
1. I have just developed a chronic headache.
2. We could not play tennis due to the rain.
3. His admittance of the mistake proves our argument.
4. It is very aggravating to break one's shoe-lace.
5. We have mutual friends: we both know Unwin and Allen.
6. You have to give a card and receive a card alternatively.
7. The event that transpired on that day was to have an effect lasting many years.
8. To show our determination, we shouted, "They will not pass!"
9. Of the three alternatives I prefer the latter. (2 misuses)
10. Dear Sir, We wish to advise you that we have today despatched the chair beside the desk which we sent yesterday. (2 misuses)
11. He seems to be very contemptible of our efforts, for he has continuously made sarcastic remarks during the last two or three weeks. (2)
12. I laid down in the sun, and this had the affect of sending me to sleep. (2)
13. They shall lend one from their neighbours if they have any sense. (2)
14. The principle of the school was not a very practicable man; he literally lived on theory, and was more uniquely lacking in observance of the rules broken by the pupils than any other man I know. (5)
15. We could not do like you advised because the amount of people in the room made it unpractical to go out between each speech; so we just lied back and waited for the next speaker. (5)

THIRD SPELLING-BEE

Geography

antarctic
artesian
canyon
cataract
hurricane
longitudinal
plateaux
prairies

Business

bankruptcy
correspondence
freight
guarantee
insolvency
liabilities
remittance
tariff

Counties

Berkshire
Denbighshire
Derbyshire
Gloucestershire
Herefordshire
Montgomeryshire
Warwickshire
Worcestershire

Creatures

aphis
boa-constrictor
budgerigar
cicada
cygnet
hippopotamus
platypus
porpoise

Politics

aristocracy
canvasser
constituency
electioneering
legislature
plebiscite
proletariat
unconstitutionally

-re

lucre
lustre
macabre
manœuvre
mediocre
reconnoitre
sceptre
sombre

-ous

auspicious
iniquitous
miscellaneous
mischievous
posthumous
prodigious
spontaneous
synonymous

Towns

Carlisle
Dolgelley
Ipswich
Leicester
Loughborough
Middlesbrough
Norwich
Torquay

Exceptions

counterfeit
fiery
paralleled
seize
shyness
truly
vying
weirdly

THIRD CHECK ON MEANINGS

Give a single word for each of the following. If correct, your
list from 1-32 will be in the reverse of alphabetical order.

1. pertaining to the spring (134) *vernal*
2. truthful (126) *veracious*
3. courteous; having refined manners (103) *urbane*
4. legendary animal with only one horn (120) *unicorn*
5. showy; gaudy (136) *tawdry*
6. to come to the help of (161) *succour*
7. one skilled in the art of war (125) *Strategist*
8. loud-voiced (108) *raucous*
9. having an acute and discerning mind (126)
10. to give up; leave behind; abandon (109)
11. foolishly chivalrous (105)
12. a play on words (156) *pun*
13. one who studies the science of the human mind (125) *psychol*
14. a plant that lasts more than two years (130) *perennial*
15. pertaining to money (133) *monetary*
16. the monetary unit of Finland (158)
17. terse; using few words (107) *laconic*
18. irrelevant; disconnected (130)
19. the science of health (107) *hygiene*
20. words pronounced alike but with different spelling and
    meaning (155) *homophones*
21. words spelt alike but with different meaning (154) *homonym*
22. twenty-one shillings (105) *guinea*
23. of giant size (123) *gigantic*
24. one who accepts all that happens as inevitable (125) *fatalist*
25. misleading; unsound (126)
26. to kill by electricity (103) *electrocute*
27. the monetary unit of Brazil (157)

174

28. used in everyday speaking (130) *colloquial*
29. belonging to corn or grain ; grains used for food (161) *cereal*
30. an easy gallop (106) *canter*
31. the part of a hall, etc., in which the hearers sit (114) *auditorium*
32. the mark * (112) *asterisk*
33. a class of mammals having a pouch for their young (43) *marsupials*
34. things added, especially at the end of books (9) *addenda*
35. knowing all things (68)
36. the science of sight (159)
37. to make vigorous (11) *invigorate*
38. to make like new (123) *renovate renew*
39. partnership in wrong-doing (143) *complicity*
40. that cannot be held back or controlled (12) *uncontrollable*
41. the stealing of another's writings (68) *plagiarism*
42. using harsh or reviling language (124)
43. liable to take fire and burn (12) *inflammable*
44. happening before the proper time (68) *premature*
45. one who bases his beliefs entirely on reason (125)
46. a woman who practises massage (13) *masseuse*
47. facts and figures collected and arranged (69)
48. keeping a firm hold (126)
49. indifferent to the sufferings of others (14)
50. the science dealing with the history of words (70) *etymology*
51. the science of motion (124)
52. belonging to the appreciation of the beautiful (66) *aesthetics*
53. a person skilled in the care of hands and feet (71) *chiropodist*
54. the act of belittling (129)
55. a list of a person's ancestors (67) *genealogy*
56. the science of language (159) *linguistics*
57. to involve (someone) in an accusation of crime (128) *implicate*
58. fond of going to law (68) *litigious*

PASSAGES FOR DICTATION AND SPEECH TRAINING

I

A capacity and taste for reading gives access to whatever has already been discovered by others. It is the key, or one of the keys, to the already solved problems. And not only so ; it gives a relish and facility for successfully pursuing the unsolved ones.

ABRAHAM LINCOLN

II

Remember when they plague you
With such words as *vague* and *ague*
That the letters don't betoken
How the words ought to be spoken ;
And that is why dictation
Can improve pronunciation.

III

Whether we shall ever rid ourselves of our superfluous consonants, like *ph* for *f*, *ck* for simple *k*, it is impossible to tell. At present we almost shudder at the American spelling *sox* for *socks*. But there is little doubt that our spelling will move onward in the direction of simplification of symbols and a more logical connexion with actual pronunciation, if only because this is the way it has always moved. If, as modern usage suggests, *often* is pronounced in standard English without its *t*, sooner or later it will lose the *t* in spelling.

G. H. VALLINS, *Words in the Making*

IV

A certified poet from Slough,
Whose methods of rhyming were rough,
Retorted, "I see
That the letters agree,
And if that's not sufficient, I'm through."

CLIFFORD WITTING, in *Punch*

V

The place of slang is in real life. There, an occasional indulgence in it is an almost necessary concession to our gregarious humanity. *Awfully nice* is an expression than which few could be sillier; but to have succeeded in going through life without saying it a certain number of times is as bad as having no redeeming vice.

H. W. & F. G. FOWLER, *The King's English*

VI

It surprises us to read of the ancient mariner listening to the birds' "sweet jargoning". But this abused and abusive word was once properly applied to the chatter of birds. Men, as they increased in presumption, supposed, as they had not sufficient wit to follow what the birds were saying, that they were not saying anything but merely babbling. So "jargon" came to mean gibberish. Now by another insulting twist it is used of the technical language of scholars, scientists or professional men. "A piece of jargon" is the synonym for "technical term". It is only when one is impatient with an expert that one is tempted to use the word, and impatience usually arises from the suspicion that he is describing in a grand manner something quite obvious.

The Times Educational Supplement

VII

Nothing can be omitted: experience drunk and experience sober, experience sleeping and experience wide-awake, experience self-conscious and experience self-forgetful, experience intellectual and experience physical, experience religious and experience sceptical, experience anxious and experience carefree, experience anticipatory and experience retrospective, experience happy and experience grieving, experience dominated by emotion and experience under self-restraint, experience in the light and experience in the dark, experience normal and experience abnormal.

A. N. WHITEHEAD, *Modes of Thought*

VIII

I tell you earnestly and authoritatively that you must get into the habit of looking intensively at words, and assuring yourself of their meaning, syllable by syllable—nay letter by letter. The study of words is called literature, and a man versed in it is called, by the consent of nations, a man of letters, instead of a man of books or of words. You might read all the books in the British Museum (if you could live long enough), and remain an utterly "illiterate" person; but if you read ten pages of a good book letter by letter, that is to say with real accuracy, you are for ever more in some measure an educated person.

JOHN RUSKIN

IX

There was a young fellow of Gloucester,
Whose wife ran away with a coucester;
  He traced her to Leicester
  And tried to arreicester,
But in spite of his efforts he loucester.

X

The English language has not only very greatly enriched its vocabulary by direct borrowing from other tongues, but has also largely availed itself of foreign aid to increase its power of forming new words. There is very little in the borrowed machinery of suffixes and prefixes that can fairly be called superfluous. Almost without exception, it has been adopted, not out of foolish affectation, but because it supplied the means of expressing necessary meanings with a degree either of precision or of brevity to which the native resources of the language were inadequate.

HENRY BRADLEY, *The Making of English*

XI

Anyone who has been brought up to speak the Anglo-American language enjoys a peculiarly favoured position. It is a hybrid. It has a basic stratum of words derived from the same stock as German, Dutch, and the Scandinavian languages. It has assimilated thousands of Latin origin. It has also incorporated an impressive battery of Greek roots. A random sample of one word from each of the first thousand pages of the *Concise Oxford Dictionary* gives the following figures: words of Romance (Latin, French, Italian, Spanish) origin, 53·6 per cent; Teutonic (Old English, Scandinavian, Dutch, German), 31·1 per cent; Greek, 10·8 per cent. With a little knowledge of the evolution of English itself, of the parallel evolution of the Teutonic languages and of the modern descendants of Latin, the American or the Briton has therefore a key to ten living European languages. No one outside the Anglo-American speech community enjoys this privilege; and no one who knows how to take full advantage of it need despair of getting a good working knowledge of the languages which our nearest neighbours speak.

FREDERICK BODMER, *The Loom of Language*

XII

The existence of the English language as a separate idiom began when Germanic tribes had occupied all the lowlands of Great Britain and when accordingly the invasions from the Continent were discontinued, so that the settlers in their new homes were cut off from that steady intercourse with their Continental relations which always is an imperative condition of linguistic unity. The historical records of English do not go so far back as this, for the oldest written texts in the English language (in "Anglo-Saxon") date from about 700 and are thus removed by about three centuries from the beginnings of the language. And yet comparative philology is able to tell us something about the manner in which the ancestors of these settlers spoke centuries before that period, and to sketch the pre-historic development of what was to become the language of King Alfred, of Chaucer and of Shakespeare.

OTTO JESPERSEN, *Growth and Structure of the English Language*

XIII

Thanks to the labours of James Murray, Henry Bradley and the many scholars who both preceded and followed them, English has now the greatest dictionary that any language has ever possessed. This dictionary (the *Oxford Dictionary*) can and should become a great instrument in higher education. The history and usage of every word known since the beginning of Middle English down to the present time are recorded with an accuracy and fulness which make our language one of the best-mapped provinces of all knowledge. It has a signal part to play in preserving the continuity of the language, and so ensuring that change may take place without debasement.

BERNARD GROOM, *A Short History of English Words*

XIV

It has been my endeavour to represent English Grammar not as a set of stiff dogmatic precepts, according to which some things are correct and others absolutely wrong, but as something living and developing under continual fluctuations.

OTTO JESPERSEN, *Modern English Grammar*

XV

The chief object in teaching grammar today—especially that of a foreign language—would appear to be to give rules which must be obeyed if one wants to speak and write the language correctly—rules which as often as not seem quite arbitrary. Of greater value, however, than this *prescriptive* grammar is a purely *descriptive* grammar which, instead of serving as a guide to what should be said or written, aims at finding out what is actually said and written by the speakers of the language investigated, and thus may lead to a scientific understanding of the rules followed instinctively by speakers and writers. Such a grammar should also be *explanatory*, giving, as far as this is possible, the reasons why the usage is such and such. These reasons may, according to circumstances, be phonetic or psychological, or in some cases both combined. Not infrequently the explanation will be found in an earlier stage of the same language : what in one period was a regular phenomenon may later become isolated and appear as an irregularity, an exception to what has now become the prevailing rule. Our grammar must therefore be *historical* to a certain extent. Finally, grammar may be *appreciative*, examining whether the rules obtained from the language in question are in every way clear (unambiguous, logical), expressive and easy, or whether in any one of these respects other forms or rules would have been preferable.

OTTO JESPERSEN, *Essentials of English Grammar*

XVI

A thing that always puzzles me—
It baffles me the more I try—
Is to determine when I'm *me*
And when I'm, strictly speaking, *I.*
The books say *I,* so it must be ;
And yet at times, oh me, oh my !
I'm absolutely sure I'm *me.*
But one solution I now know ;
It seems quite simple, you'll agree :
I'm *I* to those who want me so ;
To those that don't—well, I'm just *me.*

XVII

We must not imagine that if we have learnt how to spell and
punctuate in accordance with current conventions and how to
avoid grammatical errors, our written composition is bound
to be good. Faultless spelling and grammatical accuracy are
negative qualities only. We need to acquire them, certainly,
but once they are acquired we should forget about them, or at
any rate relegate them to the background of our consciousness.
We should try to make them, in fact, part of our second nature,
so that we do not have to think consciously about them when
we are writing.

Nothing is so likely to dam the natural flow of our thoughts
or to arrest the fluent running of our pen as over-anxious con-
cern about details of grammar or spelling. Let your pen run
freely, in pace with your thoughts if it can, though in practice
you will find it difficult to catch up with them ; then, when
your writing is done, it is time to read it through in search of
possible errors in punctuation, spelling or grammar. And to
those whose fear of making such errors cramps their style at the
beginning and induces a kind of stage fright, I would say that

on the whole it is better to have something to say and to make mistakes in saying it, than to have nothing to say and say it in faultless language.

C. E. M. JOAD, How to Write, Think and Speak Correctly

XVIII

The centipede was happy quite
Until the toad in fun
Said, "Pray which leg goes after which?"
And worked her mind to such a pitch
She lay distracted in the ditch
Considering how to run.

XIX

The habit of addressing a single person by means of a plural pronoun was decidedly in its origin an outcome of an aristocratic tendency towards class-distinction. The habit originated with the Roman Emperors, who desired to be addressed as beings worth more than a single ordinary man; and French courtesy in the middle ages propagated it throughout Europe. In England, as elsewhere, this plural pronoun (*you, ye*) was long confined to respectful address. Superior persons or strangers were addressed as *you*; *thou* thus becoming the mark either of the inferiority of the person spoken to, or of familiarity or even intimacy or affection between the two interlocutors. English is the only language that has got rid of this useless distinction. The Quakers (the Society of Friends) objected to the habit as obscuring the equality of all human beings; they therefore *thou*'d (or rather *thee*'d) everybody. But the same democratic levelling that they wanted to effect in this way, was achieved a century and half later in society at large, though in a roundabout manner, when the pronoun *you* was gradually extended to lower classes and thus lost more and more of its previous character of deference. *Thou* then for some time was reserved

for religious and literary use as well as for foul abuse, until
finally the latter use was discontinued also and *you* became the
only form used in ordinary conversation.

OTTO JESPERSEN, *Growth and Structure of the English Language*

XX

A fly and a flea in a flue
Were imprisoned, so what could they do ?
Said the fly, " Let us flee !"
" Let us fly !" said the flea,
So they flew through a flaw in the flue.

XXI

The evolution of language has been almost as unconscious as
that of an embryo. He (*man*) grasps, necessarily without reflec-
tion, this fascinating but gnarled product of evolution, neither
he nor his relatives and teachers considering at all whether the
technique of communication he is learning is modern. He is
in the position of a person who has just discovered he can ride
a bicycle and rushes off to buy the first he can find, irrespective
of whether it is new or of the latest design. It is a bicycle and
gets him along somehow, that is enough. He takes it, with all
its defects. The language he learns is the unconsidered end-
product of an evolution from the sound-communications of
ape-like ancestors. The immemorial words change less quickly
than the entities they represent, until today we find words often
extremely misleading assistants in complex thinking. A colossal
quantity of philosophizing upon every side of life is entirely
vitiated because persons use words quite unsuited to describe
the things they are discussing, as if men must always sculpture
with a hatchet because that was (perhaps) the first instrument
for the purpose.

J. G. CROWTHER, *Outline of the Universe*

XXII

Said Sir Basildon Burberry Bence,
"Your charge, sir, will hardly make sense,
For while you allege
I have broken your hedge,
I can prove you have taken offence".

STANLEY MASON

XXIII

It would be unreasonable to suppose, as is sometimes done, that the cause of the enormous propagation of the English language is to be sought in its intrinsic merits. When two languages compete, the victory does not fall to the most perfect language as such. Nor is it always the nation whose culture is superior that makes the nation of inferior culture adopt its language. It sometimes happens in a district of mixed nationalities that the population which is intellectually superior give up their own language because they can learn their neighbours' tongue while these are too dull to learn anything but their own. Thus a great many social problems are involved in the general question of rivalry of languages, and it would be an interesting, but difficult task to examine in detail all the different reasons that have in so many regions of the world determined the victory of English over other languages.

OTTO JESPERSEN, *Growth and Structure of the English Language*

XXIV

There was a young man of Japan,
Who wrote verse that never would scan.
When they said, "But the thing
Doesn't go with a swing",
He said, "Yes, but I always like to get as many
words into the last line as I can".

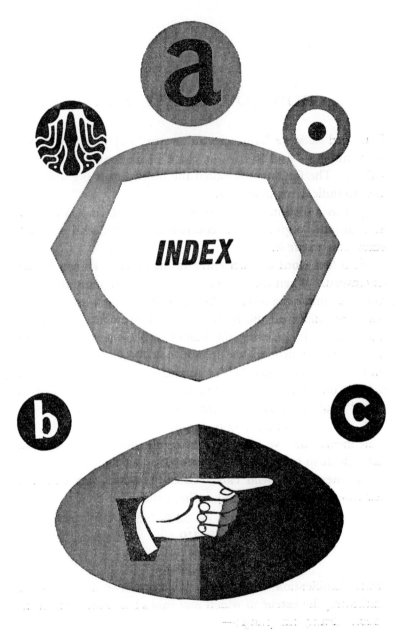

INDEX

HOW TO USE AN INDEX

THE word *index* is a Latin one and means "anything that shows or points out" and it has the same Latin root as our word *indicate*. The forefinger is called the index finger because it is used to indicate or point out.

Just as a dictionary is a guide to the words in a language, so is an index a guide to the contents of a book; and we must know how to use it.

The first word of each entry in an index is known as the catchword. When the subject of the entry is in more than one word, the main one is made the catchword. Thus, in a history book, we shall find the Battle of Waterloo under "Waterloo, Battle of". In indexing the names of persons, surnames are always placed first, so we do not look for Geoffrey Chaucer under "G" but under "C". Again, if we want to find what a book on animals has to say about wild cats, we turn to "cats", not to "wild", and find something like this:

Cats, 22, 33-6, 145-8, 183-5, 210

This means that we have to turn to all these pages and read through them before we can be sure whether there is—or is not —any mention of wild cats. Often, however, our search is narrowed by the use of sub-headings, thus:

Cats, domestic, 22, 33-6, 145-8, 210

—, Manx, 145, 210

—, Persian, 146-8

—, wild, 22, 148, 183-5

Such classification under main headings is a useful way of indicating the extent to which any subject is dealt with in the book. Study this group :—

Smith, Arthur, 14, 128-40, 269
—, John, 3, 12, 181, 190, 198
—, Sarah, 130
—, William, 3, 14, 28-48, 164-8, 210, 222, 238, 244,
    256-67

This tells us that there are four Smiths mentioned in the book
—three male and one female—and that the most frequently
mentioned, and therefore probably the most important, is
William. John, on the other hand, is only occasionally mentioned on individual pages, and although Arthur has fewer
entries than John, he is clearly more important because he has
pages 128-40 all to himself. The entry also tells us that if we
are looking for information about, say, Kenneth Smith, we shall
not find it in the book in question, but shall have to look
somewhere else.

Should we not find the page reference we seek under one
catchword, we may well find it under another, e.g. Holland
may be indexed as "Netherlands" and Farming as "Agriculture". To help us in our search, cross-references are often
used, e.g. "Holland, *see* Netherlands". Cross-references are
used also to draw attention to information supplied under other
headings. For example, the "Agriculture" entry may end
with : "*See also* Crops ; Food ; Manures".

Catchwords, sub-headings and cross-references are all to be
found in the index to this book.

Under "Greek" we have as many as seven sub-headings,
so that if, for instance, we wish to look up Greek suffixes as distinct from suffixes in general, we turn in the index to "Greek",
but if we wish to know all about suffixes as a class, we turn to
"Suffixes".

An example of a cross-reference is "Borrowing, *see* Derivatives", which shows us that words borrowed from other languages should be looked up under "Derivatives". All indexes

have to be selective, so sometimes there is no cross-reference. Here self-help will give us the answer more often than not. We wish, let us say, to learn the difference between words ending in *-ible* and those ending in *-able*, so we turn to *-ible*. The nearest we can get to it is *idiot*, which prompts us to turn to *-able*—and there it is. To paraphrase an old proverb, "If at first you don't succeed, look somewhere else".

EXERCISES

A. By using the Index, state the number of the page on which information may be found about each of the following :
 1. derivatives from the Turkish language
 2. the word *nostril*
 3. the derivation of the word *cereal*
 4. prefixes borrowed from Greek
 5. the classification of library books
 6. awkward adverbs
 7. silent consonants
 8. abstract nouns
 9. simplified spelling
 10. masculine and feminine gender

B. With the help of the Index, answer these questions :
 1. What is slang ?
 2. What is the plural of *magneto* ?
 3. What is the meaning of the technical term *antiseptic* ?
 4. From what proper noun is our modern word *silhouette* derived ?
 5. Is *connexion* or *connection* the more usual spelling ?
 6. What was the meaning of the word from which our modern word *Welsh* is derived ?
 7. What is the *homophone* of the word *write* ?
 8. From what Latin root is our modern word *erratic* derived ?
 9. Is the formation and derivation of a word called its *etymology* or its *inflexion* ?
 10. How would you show the pronunciation of the word *brochure* in phonetic symbols ?

C. Find on the first page of the Index an example of (i) a sub-heading and (ii) a cross-reference.

D. Below is an alphabetical list of items to be included in an index. Study the items carefully, then set them out in index form, grouping them where necessary under main headings. If you do this correctly there will be sixteen catchwords.

Battle of Hastings	Lord Nelson
Battleships	Lord Roberts
Charles Dickens	Matthew Matthews
Charlestown	Parmesan Cheese
County Borough of Hastings	Personal Pronouns
Dutch Cheese	Russian Poodles
Frank Jones	Short Rivers
Frenchmen	Siege of Troy
French Poodles	Sir Winston Churchill
Gorgonzola Cheese	Warren Hastings
Interrogative Pronouns	William Jones
Long Rivers	William the Conqueror

E. Below are twenty sub-headings in alphabetical order. Place four under each of these five main headings : *Astronomy, Botany, London, Physics, Poultry.*

Charing Cross	Flowers	Moon	Sound
Cockerels	Geese	Piccadilly	Strand
Constellations	Heat	Planets	Toadstools
Ducks	Herbs	Plants	Venus
Electricity	Light	Pullets	Westminster

F. Supply the missing cross-references in these index entries :

England, capital of, *see* . . .

Flora, *see* . . .

Incubation, *see* . . .

Magnetism, *see* . . .

Solar System, *see* . . .

A GENERAL QUIZ

This may be treated as further practice in using the Index or as a general test of what you have learnt from *All About English Words*. In the latter case, the Index may be used as a means of self-correction.

A. Complete each of these sentences with the right word from the brackets.
1. The American equivalent of the British *tap* is (flue, petrol, faucet, hardware).
2. The British equivalent of the American *cracker* is (firework, biscuit, holiday, bon-bon).
3. The drachma is the monetary unit of (Greece, Portugal, Russia, India).
4. The words *wait* and *weight* are (synonyms, homonyms, homophones, similes).
5. The verb to *burke* is derived from the name of a (flower, criminal, town, goddess).
6. The word *drudge* is of (Latin, Keltic, Greek, Indian) derivation.
7. (*Civvy*, *Airstrip*, *Refrigerator*) is a word that came into use during the Second World War.
8. A *carafe* usually contains (coal, beer, wine).

B. These are mixed entries from the Index. Arrange each list alphabetically as you would expect it in the Index.
1. *bête noire*, bicycle, bedlam, beneficent, belly, between, Beethoven, beside, bias
2. pronunciation, proprietary, pronouns, premature, prophecy, *poste restante*, prefixes, posthumous, principal, prepositions, preferable, practicable, practice, possessive case, portmanteau words

193

C. Answer these questions :

1. Would you classify typists as manual workers or as sedentary workers ?
2. What sort of utterance does a parrot make ?
3. What does U.N.E.S.C.O. stand for ?
4. What is the usual abbreviation for Cambridge University ?
5. What function do guide words perform in a dictionary ?
6. How did the silent b get into the word *debt* ?
7. In which world war did the word *scrounge* come into use ?
8. What special collective noun is used to name a collection of policemen ?
9. How did it come about that the English language acquired so many synonyms ?
10. Write the word *plagiarism* in phonetic symbols.
11. Are books about the English language classified under Literature or Philology in the Dewey system ?
12. What is the adjective that corresponds to the noun *Ghana* ?

D. Pick out the affix in each of the words below and say whether it comes from Old English, Latin or Greek.

1. mistrust	6. playwright	11. negligence
2. disappear	7. chemist	12. reaffirm
3. irksome	8. flexible	13. superior
4. epitaph	9. autograph	14. juvenile
5. fortitude	10. leeward	15. hemisphere

THE INDEX

ACKNOWLEDGEMENTS

Grateful acknowledgement is made of permission to include passages from the following copyright works :

Modern English Grammar and *Essentials of English Grammar* by Otto Jespersen and *The Loom of Language* by Frederick Bodmer (Messrs George Allen & Unwin Ltd.) ; *Growth and Structure of the English Language* by Otto Jespersen (Messrs Basil Blackwell and Mott Ltd.) ; *Modes of Thought* by A. N. Whitehead (Cambridge University Press) ; *A Short History of English Words* by Bernard Groom and *The Making of English* by Henry Bradley (Messrs Macmillan & Co. Ltd.) ; A limerick, *Said Sir Basildon Burberry Bence* by Stanley Masson ; *How to Write, Think and Speak Correctly* by C. E. Joad (Messrs Odhams Press Ltd.) ; *The King's English* by H. W. & F. G. Fowler (The Clarendon Press) ; A limerick, *A Certified Poet from Slough* by Clifford Witting, reproduced by permission of *PUNCH*; *Outline of the Universe* by J. G. Crowther (Messrs Routledge & Kegan Paul Ltd.) ; *The Times Educational Supplement* (The Times Publishing Company).